BEYOND
BLIND
BLAMING

STOP SOLVING THE WRONG PROBLEM
AND INSTANTLY UNLOCK RESULTS

KEVIN D. ST.CLERGY

BEFORE YOU BEGIN

——

You didn't pick up this book for tips and surface-level advice.
You picked it up because something still isn't working, even
after doing what everyone told you to do.

You've tried harder. You've blamed the usual suspects.
Hell, maybe you've even blamed yourself.

But here's the truth:
You're not failing.
You're just solving the wrong problem, and doing it really well.

This book will help you finally see what you've been missing.
And when you do? Everything changes.

Let's find the real problem and fix it for good.

CONTENTS

———

From Hero to Zero

———

HERO

WHEN I WAS TEN YEARS OLD, baseball was everything to me. I began with T-ball and worked my way up through the leagues. Throughout those years, my father always coached my team. But when my younger brother turned eight and joined the league, my dad decided to coach his team instead. I guess he figured I was well on my way and wanted to get my brother off to a good start. Unfortunately, his absence left me riddled with anxiety during practice and games, and I couldn't seem to shake it.

My father guided me through every detail and strategy of the game. He was the one who taught me how to catch and throw a ball, patiently showing me the correct grip and stance. He taught me how to swing a bat, connect with the ball, and hit confidently off a tee. He wasn't just my coach; he was the one who made me feel secure on the field. The idea of stepping onto the field without him by my side felt unfamiliar and unsettling, as if I had lost a piece of what made playing baseball so special to me. While I wanted to support my brother, I couldn't help but feel unsettled about what it would mean to play without my dad's guidance.

Though nervous about the change, I moved to the ten-year-old league with two energetic young coaches fresh out of college, who quickly made me feel at ease. After assessing my skills, I went from shortstop to second base, a change that irritated my dad, who had always positioned me at shortstop. But it proved to be the right call. My arm wasn't strong enough for those long throws from shortstop, but at second base, I thrived on the field. When it was time for me to step up to the plate to bat, I hit the ball consistently, sending it right over the second baseman's head for a base hit almost every time.

Then came our first scrimmage against the previous year's championship team. We were ready, energized from practicing, feeling strong and prepared. But things didn't go as planned. We got crushed 32 to 3. Sitting in the dugout afterward, wiping away tears, my teammates could barely look at one another. But our coaches didn't let us wallow.

Instead, they doubled down on the fundamentals—fielding, batting, teamwork. We improved steadily, as did my confidence. By season's end, my batting average was around .550—a number that would have made Babe Ruth proud. Our team kept winning, climbing toward a rematch with that same championship team. In a story that felt scripted by a baseball fairy tale, we faced the same team again in the championship game. This time, we were ready. We fought hard and won, beating the team that had once seemed unbeatable. That victory remains one of my proudest memories.

I was at the peak of my game, and people noticed. Dreams of playing for the Texas Longhorns, and maybe even the Texas Rangers, felt within reach. During the offseason, I practiced relentlessly. I covered my room with posters of my heroes, imagining myself in the big leagues with the same commanding presence. My dad and others constantly encouraged me, bragging about my dedication and potential. Overhearing conversations about my chances of playing college ball—maybe even going pro—further fueled my passion. Those ambitions became my guiding star.

ZERO

Within one year, though, everything changed. At age eleven, I stepped up to the plate, riding high on confidence. But something was different this time. I started swinging . . . and missing. From hitting almost every ball now to missing every pitch, my batting average plummeted to zero. In one season, I went from hero to zero.

It was devastating. I was doing everything right—practicing daily, pushing myself hard. Coaches and teammates pushed me harder, but my parents pushed me the hardest. I heard constant shouts from them in the stands: "Play to win this time!" "Focus!" "Try adjusting your attitude, Kevin!" Coaches echoed their feelings: "Come on! Get your head in the game." But none of their words helped to change the way I played.

COMPLETE FAILURE

Each missed swing increased my frustration. Walking back to the dugout, I saw the disappointment in the faces of the parents, who were blaming me for our losing streak. My dad's expression said it all, and I could already hear the upcoming car ride lecture before I shut the door. I knew exactly how it would go. I would hear the same old speech about how important my mindset was, how I needed to play to win, and how I had to be more aggressive on the field. Dad would probably break it down, point by point, telling me what I could have done better and what I would need to work on during practice the next day. Thinking about it made me sink into my seat a little deeper, dreading the predictable routine of critiques and pep talks that always seemed to follow every game.

The following season in the minor league—meant to prepare us for high school baseball—I wasn't even playing. Benched by the coach, I spent the entire season watching my team play the game I loved. I observed from the dugout through the chain-link fence, and my heart grew bitter. I blamed my dad for no longer being my coach and thought that change must be what had messed with my swing and my mind-set. I blamed my new coaches for being too hard on me, and then I began to blame myself. I was soon consumed with self-doubt, hatred, and betrayal. I had spent years of my life working on my baseball skills. My childhood dream was to play in high school and proudly wear a letterman's jacket. To go on to play in college and maybe even get a shot in the pros, all while watching my mom and dad in the stands and for them to see their advice and our hard work had paid off. However, life had other plans.

This was my first experience with complete failure. My dreams of following my baseball heroes—like Cal Ripken Jr., who won Rookie of the Year in 1982; or Reggie Jackson, whose effortless swing made him a home run leader—seemed to belong to a different person. I thought of legends like Wade Boggs, who was able to get on base with each at bat and dominated the league in batting average; and "the Ryan Express," Nolan Ryan, whose blazing fastballs might as well have caught fire on their way to the plate. I saw my dreams of following in their cleats slowly slip away. I kept asking myself, *How did I end up here? What am I doing wrong?*

UNCOVERING THE HIDDEN TRUTH

Two years passed like this, confined to the dugout. I kept trying, kept pushing, hoping something would change. Finally, after one last season on the sidelines, I quit baseball. The dream was dead, and I felt like a failure. Then, two weeks after my final season, I ended up at the eye doctor—not because anyone suspected a vision problem, but because my mom had scheduled a routine checkup. It was one of those fluke appointments that didn't seem important at the time. The eye doctor's words changed everything: "Sorry, kid. You're practically blind without glasses."

Suddenly, it all made sense. Those swings and misses, the frustration, the self-doubting . . . They weren't because I wasn't good enough. The truth was, I literally couldn't see the ball. No one—not my dad, my coaches, or even I—had thought of considering something as simple as my eyesight being the problem with my poor baseball performance. Looking back, it wasn't about pointing fingers or assigning blame. It was about realizing we were all so focused on the *wrong thing* that we missed the real issue entirely.

I never realized I had poor vision because it didn't seem to affect me in daily life or at school. I was a straight-A student who always sat in the front of the classroom, so I never had trouble seeing the chalkboard. I thought everything was normal. But once I got glasses, everything changed. I still remember the first time I put them on. I looked at the chalkboard and thought, *Wow, the writing is so clear now!* It was like a light bulb went off in my brain.

But the moment that stuck with me was when I saw leaves on trees for the first time. They weren't just green blobs like I'd always seen, but individual leaves, each full of detail and texture. The world came alive in a way I didn't even know I had been missing. It was a humbling, almost magical experience to realize how much I had overlooked simply because I couldn't see well.

THE UNDERLYING PROBLEM

The real issue? Throughout this journey, the adults in my life never stopped blaming me for what turned out to be beyond my control. They had me blaming myself, too, which was devastating. Sound familiar? No one saw the actual problem. Instead, they blamed everything else: my attitude, my motivation, my swing—anything but the actual cause. They pushed me harder and harder, trying to solve a problem they couldn't even diagnose.

I call this behavior Blind Blaming.™ It's at the heart of countless unresolved issues affecting people's health and personal lives, as well as organizations. It happens when people get so caught up in looking for who or what is at fault that they miss what is truly happening.

BEYOND BLIND BLAMING

My experience in baseball taught me a lesson I have carried into every challenge since: Growth and success begin when we stop blind blaming—both the harsh voices from others and our own internal critic—and start looking for the actual problem. We have to be willing to question our assumptions, to step back and see if there is something we've missed. Because sometimes the problem isn't who, where, or what we think it is.

The real breakthrough comes when we choose to be curious instead of condemning, when we seek answers instead of rushing to reprimands. It means looking at situations through fresh eyes, searching for what is working before focusing on what is not. When I started empathizing instead of disregarding—others and myself—I discovered solutions hiding in plain sight.

Sometimes we are so busy defending against external blame or beating ourselves up that we miss the actual path forward. I liken it to wearing blinders made of accusations and self-doubt. But when we finally take them off, we often find that the cage we thought we were in was partly of our own making.

The day I pulled the plug on baseball, I walked away with a new mission: to never let myself get stuck in a mental cage again—whether built by others' expectations or my own harsh judgments. I went on to hit many "home runs" in life in ways I couldn't have imagined back then—not on the baseball field but in my career.

ZERO TO HERO

In September 2022, almost forty years after my humiliating baseball season at age eleven, and after a grueling year of due diligence at work, my company was finally sold. The day it closed was one of those rare, life-changing moments. Twenty years of hard work and the emotional roller coaster of owning a business had all paid off. When the sale was official, I did something I had imagined for two decades. I took a picture off of my dream board—a picture I'd kept there all that time, representing one specific goal. I call it my "one stupid purchase." So I called my financial advisor and asked, "Well, can I get it?" He laughed and said, "Yes, Kevin, you can buy your car." I didn't wait for him to say anything else. I hung up, laughed, and headed to the dealership with that same picture in hand.

The excitement I felt was something else. I'd gotten to this moment with the help of many people along the way—mentors like David Frey, Russell Brunson, and Charlie Cook, as well as my incredible team, who'd worked just as hard (if not harder) than I did. Their support and expertise were essential, and I'll always be grateful.

I walked into the Lamborghini dealership, and the salesman, smiling, directed me to the dock where my car awaited. Looking around, I noticed a family nearby—a husband, wife, and their son, who was about thirteen years old. The boy was posing in some of the showroom cars, beaming as his parents took photos. Curious, I asked one of the employees, "What's going on?" He replied, "We encourage anyone to take photos with our cars, especially if it's for a dream board. You never know . . . Like you, they might come back one day to buy it."

That dealership was on to something! I wish more parents would help their kids dream big things—even if they seem extravagant. I approached the parents and asked if I could give their son a little something to inspire him. They agreed, so I handed him the picture that had been on my own dream board for so many years. On the back, I wrote:

Never let anyone steal your dreams.
It's hard to beat someone who never quits.

I encouraged the kid to start his own dream board with this as his first picture. I shared my story about how nearly everything I'd ever put on my dream board had come true. I'll never forget the huge smile on his face and the pride beaming from his parents. It was a bit emotional, actually. Every struggle, sacrifice, and triumph I had experienced over the years came full circle right there in the dealership. In fact, I had to step away to the bathroom to collect myself.

When I returned, an employee approached, surprised I'd given the picture away. "Weren't you going to keep that in the car with you?" he asked.

"I was," I replied. "But now it's the kid's turn to dream big."

Driving the car home was exhilarating. I'd also saved a bottle of Veuve Clicquot champagne for the occasion. A few close friends who had supported me along the way came over to join my celebration. One friend asked a question that stopped me cold.

"So, Kev, what's next?"

I laughed, thinking he was joking, but he looked serious. "I know you. You're not about to retire. You're only fifty."

"Well, I don't know," I admitted, a bit shaken.

Later that night, when the house was empty, I found myself in my office, staring at my virtual whiteboard where I kept my yearly goals. The question lingered: *What is next?* I loved what I did—coaching business owners and individuals. It never felt like work because it was deeply satisfying. But maybe it was time to reach people in a new way. I noticed a book I'd recently bought on how to give a TEDx talk. That sounded both thrilling and terrifying. I'd given talks around the world, but narrowing my message down to a single, focused, eighteen-minute talk seemed daunting.

I joined a mastermind group led by Heather Monahan, who was featured on TED.com, and after about a year of working with her and the group, she introduced me to a friend who was a speechwriter and coach. With her small team, they guided me through a process designed to uncover compelling topics. The group asked me to start by listing my biggest life lessons, a two-week exercise that was both powerful and challenging. When I shared my list with the group, one story—the baseball story—stood out. As we dove deeper, I realized I had a concept: Blind Blaming. The idea resonated with everyone. We brainstormed, refined, and crafted the speech.

Around that time, I launched a podcast and invited some successful authors and speakers as guests. After each recording, I'd ask them a small favor: "Could you take a few minutes to read my TEDx Talk draft?" They all responded positively. One person, who has experienced much success, said, "Kevin, you have a duty to write this concept as a book. It could impact millions of lives."

Excited, I went to work on this book and explored the concepts more deeply. The next year, I joined another mastermind group, the Inner Circle, led by Russell Brunson, who had helped me start the business I'd sold. At our first live meeting, I presented the concepts of Blind Blaming in a speech to him and about thirty other highly successful entrepreneurs. Afterward, Russell himself came up to me, thrilled by the concept. Others approached me, too, asking, "So, when is the book coming out? Everything you detail applies to my business, my clients, even my family."

It was incredible to see how the Blind Blaming framework resonated across different people and industries. The idea of helping millions of people move beyond misplaced blame and focus on the real problems in their lives and at work has turned into a mission for me. This book is a result of that journey, and I truly believe it has the potential to change lives. But it only works if people are willing to dig deep and do the work.

HOW THIS BOOK WILL CHANGE YOUR LIFE

My journey has shown me how easily hidden truths can hold us back, keeping us trapped in cycles of frustration without realizing what is truly stopping us. Through my work with thousands of clients in live events, coaching programs, and mastermind groups, I've seen how uncovering these truths leads to incredible breakthroughs. The insights in this book have transformed my personal relationships and career, and enhanced my opportunities for wealth and leadership. I believe they can do the same for you.

Beyond Blind Blaming offers a clear path forward through the RCD Method: Reflect, Connect, and Decide. Through extensive research and real-world application, you'll discover why traditional problem-solving often fails and how Blind Blaming keeps us trapped in negative patterns. You'll learn to identify and overcome the true obstacles to your success in business, career, finances, relationships, and personal growth—areas where you may have felt permanently stuck.

The path forward requires three fundamental shifts: release blame-based thinking, acknowledge your natural blind spots, and engage in collaborative discovery. While these principles are straightforward, their application is revolutionary. This journey demands commitment, but the rewards are profound: You will gain clarity where there once was confusion. You will experience progress where there was stagnation. And you will have breakthrough solutions to long-standing challenges.

Are you ready? Because if there is one thing I've learned, it's that we all have a choice: We can stay in the box, or we can step out and start playing our own game. Let's go!

PART ONE

AWARENESS

OUR CULTURE PECULIARLY
HONORS THE ACT OF BLAMING,
WHICH IT TAKES AS THE SIGN
OF VIRTUE AND INTELLECT.

**—Lionel Trilling, American literary critic
and short story writer**

CHAPTER 1

Understanding Blind Blaming

———

IMAGINE TRYING TO SOLVE A PUZZLE while missing half the pieces. You might spend hours attempting different combinations, growing increasingly frustrated, maybe even blaming yourself for not being clever enough—when the real problem is that you don't have all the pieces you need. This is blind blaming in action: focusing blame on the wrong things because you can't see the full picture.

WHAT IS BLIND BLAMING?

At its core, Blind Blaming is the unconscious pattern of attributing problems to the wrong causes because crucial information or insights are missing. It is "blind" because the real issue cannot be seen. It is "blaming" because we instinctively want to assign fault somewhere—even if it's to ourselves. This pattern aligns with what researchers call the "fundamental attribution error,"[1] our tendency to overemphasize personal characteristics and ignore situational factors when explaining others' behavior.

Common Blind Blaming Scenarios:

- A manager blames their team members for "not wanting to work" when they haven't bothered to define, communicate, or hire based on core values. Sixty-seven percent of performance issues stem from unclear expectations rather than employee motivation.[2]

- A parent blames their child's attitude when undiagnosed learning differences are the real challenge. According to the National Center for Learning Disabilities, 20 percent of children with learning disabilities are not diagnosed until adulthood.[3]

- An athlete blames their training program when poor sleep habits are preventing recovery. Inadequate sleep can reduce athletic performance by up to 30 percent.[4]

- A business owner blames their marketing agency when their front desk is not converting calls or texts into appointments. According to customer service research, up to 40 percent of customer conversion failures are due to internal process issues rather than marketing effectiveness.[5]

Almost every unresolved personal, workplace, or societal problem starts with people blaming the wrong thing. I'm guessing you know this is true. It's probably happening in your life or in your business right now. That's why you picked up this book. Numbers can't show how much this hurts—the stress, the wasted money, and the good workers who quit while we focus on fixing the wrong problems.

THREE FATAL FLAWS OF BLIND BLAMING

1. Blind Blaming Feels Right

Brenda was confident she knew why her audiology and hearing aid practice was struggling: *I need better marketing.* It made perfect sense. Better marketing would mean new private-pay patients, revenue, and success. She invested thousands in ads and rebranding only to face the same problems with a dwindling bank account.

This is the most dangerous aspect of blind blaming; it feels completely logical. When we can't see the real problem, our explanations make perfect sense based on the information we have. This aligns with the "availability heuristic": We believe explanations that come to mind easily, regardless of their accuracy.[6]

Brenda's story perfectly illustrates how blind blaming creates a dangerous feedback loop. While she poured resources into marketing with little or no success, she constantly switched marketing companies and blamed them for her failures. At the same time, her business's true challenge lay hidden: Her front desk team answered only 50 percent of incoming calls, and those rare conversations failed to convert due to poor appointment-setting practices. Like a shadow-boxing match, Brenda fought the wrong opponent while her actual problems grew unchecked. The "logical" marketing explanation drained her finances and shielded her from discovering the real issues eroding her patient relationships—creating a costly lesson in the price of misplaced certainty.

2. Blind Blaming Is Self-Reinforcing

James was convinced his team's productivity problem stemmed from the mentality of, *Nobody wants to work anymore.* Whenever someone didn't do what he asked of them, missed a deadline, or communication broke down, he added it to his mental list of "proof." He then logged into a private Facebook group and wrote a long post about how nobody wants to work anymore and that he has the toughest time finding good employees.

The flood of sympathetic comments and similar stories from other business owners reinforced his belief, creating an echo chamber of shared frustration. This social validation made him even more resistant to examining his management style, hiring strategy, onboarding processes, and core values—or considering alternative explanations.

When presented with examples of highly engaged teams or successful modern workplaces, he dismissed them as rare exceptions that only proved his rule. With each month, his certainty grew stronger, even as his team's performance declined—a perfect demonstration of how self-reinforcing blind blaming creates its reality.

Once we decide on a cause for our problems, we seek evidence confirming our belief. This creates a self-reinforcing cycle that psychologists call "confirmation bias":[7]

- We identify a supposed cause.
- We find evidence that supports our explanation.
- We dismiss or ignore contrary evidence.
- Our belief becomes stronger.
- We become more resistant to alternative explanations.

These self-reinforcing cycles become nearly impossible to break without outside intervention. In James's case, each perceived failure was like another brick in the wall, slowly building up his defenses against self-awareness. Every missed deadline and communication breakdown reinforced his *nobody wants to work* narrative, creating an impenetrable psychological fortress.

Like the famous Pink Floyd song, "Another Brick in the Wall," James constructed a mental barrier, brick by brick, that blocked out any chance for critical self-reflection. But unlike the song's haunting call to break down the wall, James seemed content to let it stand, shielding himself from the uncomfortable truth that the problem might not lie entirely with others. The actual issues buried beneath his blame were his reactive hiring practices, nonexistent onboarding and certification program, unclear company values, and authoritarian management style that drove away talent.

However, like a detective convinced of the wrong suspect, the more evidence James collected about "lazy workers," the less capable he became of seeing his role in the story. This demonstrates how self-reinforcing blame doesn't just hide problems; it actively prevents their solution.

3. Blind Blaming Blocks Real Solutions

While we're focused on the wrong problem, we can't solve the right one. This creates organizational blind spots that can persist for years, leading to:

- Wasted time and resources
- Growing frustration
- Damaged relationships
- Lost opportunities
- Diminished confidence

Consider Emma, a talented chef who poured three years and her life savings into her struggling restaurant. As profits remained elusive, she cycled through a carousel of explanations: Her location wasn't prime enough. Her prices weren't competitive enough. Her marketing wasn't reaching the right people. Her city's "food culture" wasn't sophisticated enough. Each new theory led to costly changes and adaptations, depleting her resources and energy.

Yet the real issue could be found on every customer's plate: Her portion sizes had quietly shrunk while prices remained high, creating a value disconnect that drove customers away. A simple adjustment could have aligned her portions with customer expectations, transforming complaints into compliments and losses into profits. Instead, blind blaming kept her searching in all the wrong places until her dream of restaurant ownership slipped away. A stark reminder that the most expensive problems are often the ones we refuse to see.

THE PSYCHOLOGY BEHIND BLIND BLAMING

Think of blind blaming as a mental magic trick that fools even the most intelligent people. Just like a magician directs your attention away from how the trick works, our minds can steer us toward comfortable answers instead of true ones. We must peek behind the curtain and see how our brains create this illusion in order to stop falling for this trick.

The Illusion of Control

Jackson sat in his home office, surrounded by a graveyard of abandoned planners, productivity books, and a mountain of unpaid bills. As he meticulously transferred his tasks into yet another new system—his fifth this year—he fought to stay focused through his usual afternoon mental fog. *This time*, he thought, *I've finally found the solution that will make everything click.* The divorce papers on his desk told a different story though. His wife's final straw had been discovering her health insurance had lapsed, another victim of Jackson's chronic forgetfulness and missed payments.

This unwavering belief in our ability to control outcomes, what psychologist Ellen Langer termed the "illusion of control," runs deep in human nature. Her research revealed how persistently we overestimate our influence, even in situations governed purely by chance.[8] This illusion manifested as an endless search for Jackson's perfect productivity system. His business partner had even hired an ADHD coach to help him stay on track—another expensive solution that didn't solve the problem.

It wasn't until a routine checkup that the real issue emerged. When his doctor asked, "So you've been dealing with ADHD your whole life?" Jackson said, "No, I haven't. And I wish people would stop saying that!" Her unexpected response changed everything: "Then I think there's something more significant at play here. You might have sleep apnea." A subsequent sleep study revealed the truth. His brain wasn't getting enough oxygen. This disruptive sleep disorder was causing him to feel mentally exhausted and unable to focus, no matter how many productivity systems he tried.

The illusion of control pattern occurs because our brains are wired to seek control and certainty, even at the cost of accuracy. When faced with challenges, we instinctively grab onto explanations that suggest we can fix things through sheer effort or better choices. It's more comforting to believe we chose the wrong productivity system than to consider an invisible health condition that might be dismantling our lives.

COGNITIVE BIASES

Our brains are wired with shortcuts that can lead us astray. Cognitive biases are systematic patterns of deviation from rational judgment that occur due to limitations in human information processing and memory. These mental shortcuts, or heuristics, while often helpful in making quick decisions, can lead to systematic errors in reasoning, evaluation, and interpretation of information. Our brains have evolved these short-cuts to help us process the vast amount of information we encounter daily. But in modern contexts, they can impair our ability to make objective decisions and form accurate judgments.

There are three types of cognitive biases that operate largely on an unconscious level, affecting everything from how we perceive ourselves and others to how we make business, financial, and personal decisions, even when we're aware of their existence.

1. **Confirmation Bias**: Once we believe in something, we become treasure hunters, obsessed with finding proof we are right. In business, if we decide "marketing is the problem," every slow month becomes another gold coin in our proof chest. In our personal lives, this same bias shows up when we convince ourselves someone doesn't like us. Suddenly, every brief text or canceled plan becomes "evidence," while we ignore their genuine attempts to connect. Just like a business owner skipping marketing review calls to avoid contradicting data, we might stop reaching out to that friend entirely, creating a self-fulfilling prophecy. Be it relationships or revenue, we are twice as likely to dig for proof that we are right than to search for evidence that we might be wrong.[9]

2. **Self-Serving Bias**: This cognitive bias emerges when we pat ourselves on the back for wins but blame outside factors for losses. Think of a sales team that credits their skill when deals close but blames marketing when they don't. This plays out in our personal

finances too. We credit our investment wisdom when stocks rise but blame the market when they fall. In relationships, we often take credit for good times while blaming our partner during rough patches. Research shows we do this everywhere in life, taking credit for good results 70 percent more often than bad ones—in our businesses, bank accounts, or bonds with others.[10]

3. **Availability Bias**: With this bias, our minds grab the first explanation within reach, like someone frantically searching a dark room but only looking where the flashlight beam lands. In business, when we lose one sale over the price, we immediately assume we need to lower prices. In relationships, when one person ghosts us on a dating app, we quickly conclude something must be wrong with our profile picture. Business leaders and individuals alike consistently overweigh recent, vivid experiences while missing deeper patterns. We'll spend months adjusting our pricing strategy or obsessing over our dating profiles while ignoring fundamental issues like poor sales processes or communication patterns. The easy answer feels right because it's right there, but like a magician's misdirection, it keeps us from seeing the real problem hiding in the shadows.

BEHAVIORAL BEDROCK

When the illusion of control intertwines with our cognitive biases, it creates what I call a behavioral bedrock—layers of self-reinforcing beliefs that harden over time like sedimentary rock. Each layer builds upon the last: Our confirmation bias selectively collects evidence that supports our chosen solution, our self-serving bias protects us from considering our role in the problem, and our availability bias keeps us fixated on surface-level explanations. Like Jackson with his productivity systems, we sink deeper into familiar but ineffective solutions. Each failed attempt paradoxically strengthens our commitment to the wrong path.

This hardened bedrock of beliefs becomes increasingly difficult to pierce, making us resistant to alternative explanations or solutions that might actually address the root cause. The more time and emotional energy we invest in our chosen narrative, the more we filter reality through these distorted lenses, creating a self-perpetuating cycle that can take years or even decades to break. Only by recognizing how these psychological forces work together can we begin to chip away at this behavioral bedrock and open ourselves to more accurate—if less comfortable—explanations for our challenges.

RECOGNIZING BLIND BLAMING IN YOUR LIFE

We all have blind spots in our rearview mirror—areas where danger lurks beyond our vision. Blind blaming works the same way, shaping our decisions and derailing our progress while remaining conveniently out of sight. I believe that true change begins with awareness. But how do you spot something that is designed to stay hidden? The key lies in recognizing its telltale tracks—the patterns, behaviors, and recurring frustrations that signal blind blaming at work in your life.

These tracks appear across every domain: in our careers, where we blame market conditions instead of examining our business practices; in our relationships, where we attribute conflicts to our partner's flaws rather than our communication patterns; in our parenting, where we fault our children's attitudes instead of our inconsistent boundaries; and in our personal growth, where we blame circumstances for our stalled progress instead of confronting our resistance to change.

Before you invest in another erroneous solution, see if you recognize any of these warning signs:

1. Recurring Problems

Studio executives huddled together for another emergency meeting, staring at disappointing box office numbers. "It's superhero fatigue," they declared, blaming audiences for losing interest. Their solution? Make their serious superhero films more comedic, add more jokes, get more creative with CGI, create more jaw-dropping moments. But even after implementing these "great" ideas, ticket sales fell further with each new movie release.

Up to 85 percent of recurring problems stem from misidentified root causes.[11] The studios blamed "superhero fatigue" when the real issue was straying from what made these movies successful in the first place: compelling stories about complex heroes we grew up with who were treated with respect and emotional depth. Audiences weren't tired of superheroes; they were tired of their beloved characters being turned into punchlines.

Look for these signs:

- You face the same challenges repeatedly.
- Solutions provide temporary relief, but the problems return.
- You feel stuck in a cycle of blame and failure.

2. Escalating Frustration

Sarah stared at her workout and nutrition log, her chest tightening with frustration and disappointment. Six months—*six grueling months*—of relentless training: waking up at four a.m. to sprint intervals, running hills, lifting weights, and repeatedly pushing her body to failure. She had also followed her nutrition plan exactly as her coach had planned. However, regardless of her best efforts and dedicated routine, her race times were getting slower and slower. Her hands trembled as her spirit sank. Yet another day of training to exhaustion and seeing no positive results.

It made no sense. The more she trained and the harder she worked, the *slower* her time became. A lump formed in her throat, and her heart ached as negativity crept in: *I might not be good enough to compete.* She didn't know that it wasn't her lack of running ability or stamina holding her back; overtraining was silently undoing her work. Her body was breaking down, and she never had time to recover. It can be easy to blame ourselves when things go wrong instead of questioning the approach we've been taking all along. Persistent frustration often signals a misalignment between the perceived cause and the actual cause.

Be on the lookout for these scenarios:

- Your efforts to improve yield diminishing returns.
- You are working harder but seeing less progress.
- Solutions that should work don't work.

3. Relationship Strain

Mark couldn't understand why his wife seemed defensive whenever he raised concerns about their spending. He saw that they consistently spent more monthly while their income remained unchanged: $55 for food delivery. $83 for the nail salon. $124 for the latest streaming service. The monthly expenses kept piling up. While each transaction seemed relatively small, they turned into a mountain of debt over time.

Mark prided himself on being direct about money, yet every conversation about their budget turned into an argument. "She's just being too emotional about this," he decided, missing how his constant lectures and financial micromanagement made her feel judged and controlled. The more she withdrew, the more he doubled down on tracking every purchase and criticizing her spending, creating a spiral of resentment and distance. Misattribution of blame appears in 80 percent of failing relationships.[12]

How to assess if your blind blaming is affecting your relationships:

- People around you seem defensive.
- Communication breaks down.
- Trust erodes despite good intentions.

4. Diminishing Confidence

Jennifer had built a successful career as a speaker and coach, regularly filling rooms of 300 people. Lately, her event numbers were dropping to 150, then 100. *Maybe I'm losing my touch*, she worried, putting her focus on creating new content and spending hours rewriting her presentations. Each event felt more challenging than the last, leading her to slash prices and overdeliver with longer sessions and endless bonus materials. *I must be getting stale*, she thought, not realizing that the fear of adapting her business model was the real problem.

While she blamed her speaking skills, the market had shifted, and her customers now preferred intimate, high-ticket group programs rather than large events—a change she refused to consider. When we misattribute the source of our struggles, our confidence erodes in proportion to our misconceptions.

Be mindful when:

- You question your abilities more frequently.
- Your self-doubt increases over time.
- You feel less capable of managing a situation than you did in the past.

5. Supportive Sabotage

Mike stood on the sidelines watching his daughter's soccer game, becoming increasingly frustrated. "You need to be more aggressive!" he shouted as she hesitated near the ball. "You're playing too scared!" After each game, he'd list everything she needed to fix, convinced his criticism would toughen her up and make her a better player. Meanwhile, his daughter's love for the sport slowly faded, along with her self-confidence.

The root of the issue was not her so-called timid play style but her lack of proper ball control training, which left her hesitant during games. His attempt to help only addressed the surface problem while unintentionally creating new ones. This reflects a broader trend in youth sports:

"Seven out of ten young athletes quit organized sports by age thirteen, with well-intentioned parental criticism cited as the primary cause."[13]

Be aware of how others sabotage you:

- They offer constant "helpful" criticism.
- Their solutions focus on your perceived character flaws.
- Their help leaves you feeling worse, not better.

THE HIGH COST OF MISSING HIDDEN TRUTHS

When we miss the hidden truths in our lives, the costs cascade through every vital dimension: Our health falters, our wealth diminishes, relationships become strained, our leadership effectiveness erodes—costing companies billions of dollars—and communities fragment. Rather than recognizing these subtle but crucial signals, we often default to blind blaming: pointing our finger away from us and onto circumstances, others, or systems.

The following stories reveal the steep price of overlooking the truths we have become blind to and how our habit of blind blaming keeps us trapped, blocking the very insights that could transform our circumstances.

Complete Meltdown

A successful CEO, Brooke watched helplessly as every area of her life seemed to spiral downward simultaneously. She blamed market conditions for falling sales, her husband's "neediness" for their marriage strain, her team's "lack of drive" for missed targets, and herself for failing to muscle through it all. The real root cause—her unmanaged anxiety—was silently destroying everything she had worked so hard to build. Leadership problems rarely travel alone.

With each new challenge, Brooke's pattern of blame became more entrenched, creating a fortress of finger-pointing that kept real solutions at bay. Her constant state of fight-or-flight left her exhausted yet unable to rest, trapped in a cycle of reacting without truly addressing what lay beneath. Like many leaders facing compound stressors, she was approaching emotional bankruptcy—that critical point where the mind simply refuses to process one more crisis, one more explanation, one more Band-Aid solution.

It wasn't until a key client quietly took their business elsewhere that Brooke finally hit pause. No matter how resilient, the human system can only sustain prolonged stress without resolution for so long before it begins to shut down. Her tendency to blame external factors had become a security blanket, protecting her from having to face the uncomfortable truth: She needed help learning to manage her anxiety in healthier ways. Only by stepping back to assess the real patterns at play could she begin to chart a path forward—one that would require as much inner work as business strategy.

Through work with an executive coach, a mastermind group, and a therapist, Brooke gradually learned to recognize her anxiety signals before they escalated into crisis-level reactions. She implemented daily meditation and regular exercise while developing a more balanced approach to leadership that embraced vulnerability and open communication with her husband as well as her team. As her anxiety became more manageable, her business metrics, marriage, and team dynamics naturally began to improve—proving that sometimes the most powerful leadership tool is the courage to look within.

Health

Cynthia stared at her reflection in frustration, her shoulders slumping as exhaustion washed over her. Dark circles under her eyes hinted at sleepless nights spent scrolling through fitness TikToks and reading Reddit posts about "proven weight-loss techniques," desperately searching for answers. Despite consistently working out and being assisted by three elite trainers for the past two years, spending thousands on supplements, and religiously following every new diet trend, nothing seemed to work.

Her energy was at an all-time low, and the scale refused to budge more than the initial two pounds. With tears in her eyes, she thought, *Why can't I figure this out? What is wrong with me?* And the familiar sting of failure settling in. Her inner voice began its harsh and unforgiving lies: *I just need to work harder, be more focused, and do the work!* She masked her frustration with determination as she pushed through another punishing workout, even though her body begged for rest. It wasn't until a functional medicine doctor tested her hormones that the real problem emerged: Her testosterone levels were critically low. Within months of starting hormone pellet therapy, her energy soared, and her body finally responded to training. This highlights a larger issue: As much as 70 percent of women's health issues are initially misdiagnosed as lifestyle or effort problems.[14]

Wealth

Marcus watched his friends building wealth—working reasonable hours, growing their savings, investing wisely—while he seemed trapped in an endless cycle of working harder and not reaping the same financial rewards. Despite matching their income, his bank account remained stubbornly empty. He blamed it on the cost of doing business and market conditions, missing the real drain on his finances: his untracked spending and lack of basic budgeting. While his friends made informed financial decisions based on precise numbers, Marcus was flying blind, racking up debt, living a lifestyle he couldn't afford, and using his business as a cash machine. His wealth-building efforts were undermined by thousands of small, unmonitored expenses that added up to a fortune over time.

Like many people, Marcus was paying a steep price for avoiding honest self-reflection. The time and energy spent defending his financial choices and blaming external factors could have been invested in creating real solutions. Instead, his reluctance to face the numbers head-on kept him locked in a pattern of reactionary decisions and mounting stress. The truth was uncomfortably simple: No amount of hard work could outpace his unexamined poor financial habits. Only by stepping back to take a clear-eyed look at his spending patterns could he begin to build the wealth he had worked so hard to create.

Marcus finally confronted his spending patterns through a sobering session with a financial advisor who laid bare his real numbers. He implemented strict budgeting software, separated his personal and business accounts, and began treating his finances with the same analytical rigor his successful friends applied. Within eighteen months, his newfound financial discipline transformed his bank balance from empty to growing steadily—proving that awareness and systematic habits, not just hard work, are the true engines of wealth building.

Relationships

Lisa sat across from her marriage counselor, listing the communication failures of Adam, her husband, while he cataloged her emotional reactions. Neither saw how their financial insecurity was creating the tension they blamed on each other. Their family business would pay the price for this blind spot.

Beneath their surface conflicts lay a deeper truth: Both were desperately seeking security and validation, core needs that their financial stress had left chronically unmet. Instead of recognizing these fundamental requirements for stability and connection, they continued to mistake symptoms for causes, and their relationship and business both suffered from this misalignment. It's no surprise that seven out of ten relationship conflicts in business-owning families stem from misunderstood core needs.[15]

Through dedicated couples counseling and financial planning sessions, Lisa and Adam learned to see their conflicts through the lens of shared goals rather than personal attacks. By addressing their financial insecurity head-on with a clear business strategy and household budget, they discovered that their core needs for security and validation could be met through partnership rather than opposition. Their business began to thrive as their relationship healed, proving that personal and professional growth often go hand in hand.

KEY TAKEAWAYS

- Blind blaming is the unconscious pattern of attributing problems to the wrong causes because crucial information or insights are missing. It is "blind" because the real issue cannot be seen. It is "blaming" because we instinctively want to assign fault somewhere—even if it's to ourselves.
- Blind blaming is a natural human tendency or bad habit, backed by decades of cognitive psychology research.
- Recognition of the pattern is the first step to breaking it.
- Systematic questioning of our assumptions leads to better solutions.

REFLECTION QUESTIONS

1. Think about a recurring challenge in your life. What explanations have you accepted for why it persists?

....

....

....

....

....

2. When was the last time you discovered that a problem had a completely different cause than what you initially believed?

....

....

....

....

....

3. In what areas of your life do you feel stuck despite significant efforts to improve?

....

....

....

....

....

4. How might your current explanations for challenges limit your ability to see alternative solutions?

....

....

....

....

....

ACTION STEPS

1. **Choose one area of your life where you feel stuck.**
   - Make it specific and current.
   - Write it down.

....

....

....

....

2. **List all the factors you currently blame or complain about for the situation.**
   - Be honest with yourself.
   - Include everything, no matter how small.

....

....

....

....

3. **Ask yourself: "What if I'm missing something important?"**
   - Sit with this question.
   - Let yourself be curious, not judgmental.

4. **Write down three alternative explanations you haven't considered.**

   - Push yourself beyond the obvious.
   - Consider perspectives that make you uncomfortable.

....

....

....

....

....

Remember: The goal isn't to stop assigning responsibility. The goal is to ensure you are addressing the real issues rather than wasting energy on misplaced blame.

LOOKING AHEAD

In the next chapter, we'll discover how blame and complaint act as invisible anchors, holding you back from your true potential and draining the very energy you need to create positive change. You'll learn a practical formula for transforming these patterns into stepping stones toward possibility.

The challenge isn't that you handle your difficulties poorly; it's that you've been focusing your attention in the wrong direction. Real transformation begins when you shift from asking, "Who is at fault?" to "What is possible from here?"

Take a moment to consider: *What opportunities might I discover if I could redirect the energy I currently spend on blaming and complaining?*

66

DISCONTENT, BLAMING,
COMPLAINING, SELF-PITY CANNOT
SERVE AS A FOUNDATION FOR A
GOOD FUTURE,
NO MATTER HOW MUCH EFFORT
YOU MAKE.

**—Eckhart Tolle, spiritual teacher and
self-help author**

99

CHAPTER 2

Negativity to Possibility

——

THE JOURNEY FROM STAGNATION TO SUCCESS begins with a fundamental shift in how we respond to challenges. When we release our grip on blame and complaints, we free up the mental and emotional energy needed to spot opportunities, solve problems, and create real change. This transformation isn't just about positive thinking; it's about replacing unproductive habits with powerful tools for growth. As we'll explore in this chapter, those who master this shift discover something remarkable: The very obstacles they once blamed for holding them back became the foundation for their greatest achievements. The path forward opens up not when circumstances change but when we change.

THE HARD TRUTH ABOUT BLAMING AND COMPLAINING

Before diving into solutions, we need to confront an uncomfortable truth: Blaming and complaining are addictive. They offer temporary relief, like a pressure valve releasing steam. They can even feel justified. After all, sometimes others really are at fault, and situations really are unfair. But here's what successful people know: Being right about who or what's at fault won't get you where you want to go.

Jack Canfield, in *The Success Principles*, advocates for taking 100 percent responsibility for your life.[1] Jocko Willink and Leif Babin promote "extreme ownership" in their work.[2] These principles have transformed countless lives and organizations. But there is a nuanced truth we need to acknowledge: While we can't control everything that happens to us, we can control our responses.

Think about it this way: If you're stuck in traffic, you are not the one who caused the accident ahead. You are not responsible for the decisions of other drivers. But you are 100 percent responsible for how you handle the delay. Will you spend that time complaining and raising your blood pressure? Or will you use it productively, perhaps listening to an audiobook or planning your day? You can't claim responsibility for things beyond your control, but you can recognize that your response to every situation shapes its ultimate impact on your life.

THE HIDDEN COST OF BLAMING AND COMPLAINING

In nature, animals focus on what is ahead. A cheetah doesn't blame the gazelle that got away or complain about the heat. It conserves energy and prepares for the next opportunity. Yet humans often do the opposite. We react instinctively, letting emotions drive our responses. Instead of moving forward, we get stuck in a reactive cycle of pointing fingers and listing grievances, burning valuable energy that could be used for solutions.

When we are reactive, we spiral into an exhausting loop: Something goes wrong, we blame others or ourselves, we complain about the situation, and we stay locked in that negative state. This reactionary pattern becomes a self-fulfilling prophecy, creating more problems to react to. Every blame statement locks us in the past, and every complaint anchors us to what is wrong. Like an animal pacing in circles instead of exploring its habitat to hunt, we trap ourselves in patterns that prevent results, growth, and happiness.

On top of the emotional cost, research shows that chronic complaining:

- Rewires neural pathways toward negativity
- Increases stress hormones
- Weakens immune function
- Strains relationships
- Blocks creative problem-solving[3]

When we are caught in this cycle, we literally train our brains to spot problems instead of opportunities. Like wearing dark glasses, we dim our view of potential solutions.

THE AGENCY CRISIS: MY BIG LESSON

The day we faced a revenue crisis at our digital marketing agency in 2009 taught me everything about blame, complaint, and the power of focusing on solutions. A perfect storm had hit: Bad hires were underperforming, client marketing budgets were shrinking due to economic uncertainty, and Google's latest algorithm changes had essentially set everyone back to square one. Our clients were not just complaining; they were leaving.

I spiraled into a cycle of blame, pointing fingers at our employees for missing deadlines, at our partners for poor communication, at our marketing team for not bringing in enough leads, and at myself for being a failure as a leader. The more I blamed, the deeper the team sank into a pit of negativity and lost opportunities.

Then I watched Charlie, my business partner and our voice of reason. While everyone else was caught in the spiral of despair and finger-pointing, he stayed focused on what we could actually control. He saw past the surface problems to what really mattered: creating an exceptional experience for both our employees and our clients. Instead of obsessing over rankings and metrics that weren't driving real results, Charlie steered us toward measuring what truly mattered—leads generated and actual business growth for our clients. Something that business still focuses on today, even though I don't own it anymore.

Charlie didn't waste energy on blame or complaints. Instead, he focused on a solution, transforming our agency's entire approach. We shifted from chasing algorithms to delivering meaningful business impact. This wasn't just about surviving a crisis. It was about building a stronger, more resilient agency that prioritizes results. This simple shift in perspective became my blueprint for handling every challenge that followed.

THE INSIGHT-IMPLEMENTATION MATRIX: UNDERSTANDING YOUR STARTING POINT

It is crucial to understand where you currently stand in relation to negative patterns. The Insight-Implementation Matrix reveals how you typically respond to challenges by mapping two critical capabilities: your ability to recognize patterns of blame and complaint (insight), and your capacity to take constructive action (implementation).

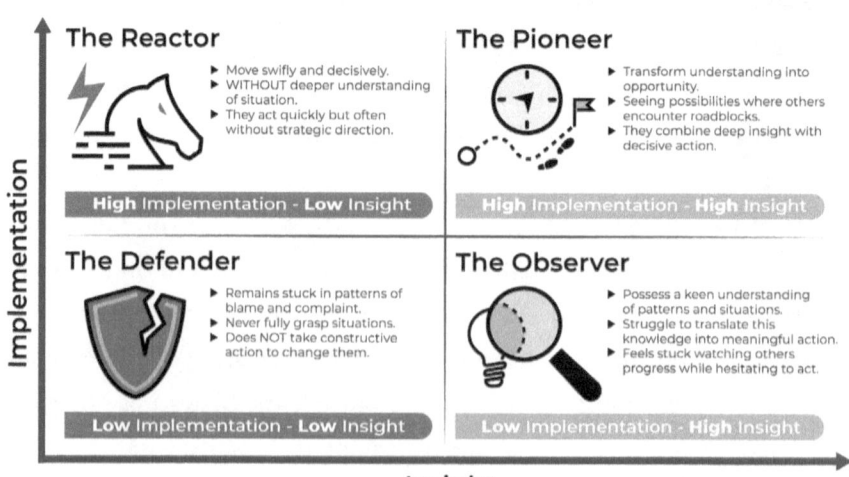

THE INSIGHT-IMPLEMENTATION MATRIX

The Reactor
- Move swiftly and decisively.
- WITHOUT deeper understanding of situation.
- They act quickly but often without strategic direction.

High Implementation - **Low** Insight

The Pioneer
- Transform understanding into opportunity.
- Seeing possibilities where others encounter roadblocks.
- They combine deep insight with decisive action.

High Implementation - **High** Insight

The Defender
- Remains stuck in patterns of blame and complaint.
- Never fully grasp situations.
- Does NOT take constructive action to change them.

Low Implementation - **Low** Insight

The Observer
- Possess a keen understanding of patterns and situations.
- Struggle to translate this knowledge into meaningful action.
- Feels stuck watching others progress while hesitating to act.

Low Implementation - **High** Insight

Implementation

Insight

Like a compass showing your current location, the Insight-Implementation Matrix places you in one of four positions:

- **Pioneers** combine high insight with strong implementation. They recognize negative patterns quickly and actively work to transform them into opportunities.

- **Observers** have strong insight but struggle with implementation. They clearly see what needs to change but often get stuck in analysis paralysis.

- **Reactors** take quick action but lack deeper insight. They make changes without understanding root causes, often repeating the same patterns.

- **Defenders** resist both insight and implementation. They stay locked in familiar negative patterns, defending the status quo even when it is not serving them.

While we all start in different quadrants, the goal is clear: to develop the traits of a Pioneer. What sets Pioneers apart isn't natural talent or luck but their ability to combine deep awareness with purposeful action. They have mastered the art of turning negative patterns into opportunities for growth. When you study successful Pioneers across different fields and situations—from business leaders to educators to healthcare professionals, to individuals and couples—you find they all share a common approach: They have an ability to spot patterns and transform them into possibilities. So how do we move forward, regardless of our starting point? Through what I call the ACT Formula.

AWARENESS + CHOICE + TRANSFORM = POSSIBILITIES

THE ACT FORMULA

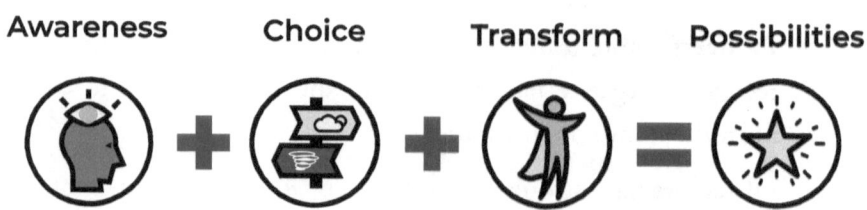

The ACT Formula offers the antidote to reactionary behavior. Instead of getting caught in the blame-and-complain cycle, it provides a clear path forward. This formula represents a systematic approach to personal growth. First is developing an Awareness of our thoughts and patterns. Second is making a conscious Choice about our responses. Third is taking actions that Transform our relationship to challenges. The result is an expansion of Possibilities in our lives. This is not a feel-good acronym. It is a practical pathway from reaction to action, from negative patterns into possibilities. Let me show you how it works:

1. Awareness: Catching Yourself in the Act

Think of *awareness* as your early warning system. Like a skilled detective, you learn to spot the subtle clues that you're slipping into negativity. The tightness in your shoulders when a team member makes a mistake. The familiar surge of frustration when your spouse leaves dishes in the sink. The reflexive "Yes, but . . ." or " No, that will never work because . . ." response when someone offers a suggestion.

Barbara, a CEO I worked with, described her awareness moment perfectly: "I was midway through my usual rant about our marketing team when I caught my reflection in the conference room window. My face was twisted in frustration. My hands were clenched. My whole body radiated negativity. I saw what I was doing for the first time—not just to the team, but to myself."

This is awareness in action—not judging, not fixing, just noticing. It's like turning on a light in a dark room. Suddenly, you can see what has been there all along.

Here are the key elements of developing this awareness:

- Recognize when you are blaming and complaining.
- Notice your negative thought patterns and reactions.
- Observe how negativity affects your energy and outcomes.
- Identify your triggers for negative spirals.
- Spot when you become focused on problems instead of possibilities.
- Note where you are in the Insight-Implementation Matrix

2. Choice: The Power Pause

The magic happens in the milliseconds after awareness kicks in—during that crucial pause between trigger and reaction. This is where choice enters the equation. The intentional pause between stimulus and response holds more power than most people realize. It's the difference between being a puppet of your patterns and becoming the author in charge of your story.

Remember James from chapter 1? When his biggest client threatened to leave, his automatic response would have been to blame his team who "didn't want to work" and fire off an angry email. Instead, he caught himself (awareness), took a deliberate pause, and chose differently. "I felt the usual anger rising," he told me. "But this time I did something different. I paused, set my phone down, and asked myself: *What possibility am I missing here?*"

This is the power of the pause. It creates space for choice. Instead of forcing positivity or suppressing emotions, it allows you to pause long enough to look for possibilities even when—*especially when*—negativity feels justified.

The pause looks different for everyone. Maria, a busy mother of three, found her pause during morning carpool when her daughter announced she had forgotten her science project. Instead of launching into her usual lecture, she took three deep breaths. That small pause helped her see an opportunity to teach all of her kids problem-solving skills instead of rein-forcing shame in her daughter. Whether you are dealing with workplace challenges, family dynamics, or personal setbacks, the power pause gives you the space to choose your response.

Here are practical ways to create that crucial space between trigger and response:

- When your first instinct is to blame your partner for miscommu-nication, pause and take three deep breaths. Ask yourself: "What might they be experiencing right now?"

- Before complaining about your health setbacks, create a thir-ty-second pause. Use this moment to ask: "What one small action can I take today to support my well-being?"

- When facing financial pressure, resist the urge to blame the econ-omy or your job. Instead, take a quiet moment to ask: "Where do I have room to make different choices?"

- If you catch yourself complaining about family dynamics, pause mid-sentence. Redirect with: "What understanding am I missing here? What could I do differently?"

Before joining a complaint session (at work, with friends, or online), wait ten seconds. Use this brief pause to ask: "How could I steer this toward solutions instead?"

3. Transform: Where Possibility Becomes Reality

This stage is where the rubber meets the road. Transform is the active ingredient that turns awareness and choice into tangible results. It's one thing to notice negativity and choose a different response. It's even more powerful to then transform that energy into active, forward momentum.

Michelle, a restaurant owner, demonstrated this beautifully during the height of the pandemic. When most owners complained about restric-tions (awareness), she chose to look for opportunities (choice). Then, she transformed that perspective into action, creating a revolutionary out-door dining experience that saved and expanded her business. "Every time I caught myself complaining, I transformed it into a question: How could this challenge become an opportunity?"

When you practice the power pause consistently, you can transform negative patterns into constructive action. Let's break down the process of awareness to positive change:

- Take small, immediate steps toward the possibilities you have identified, whether at home or work.

- Transform complaints into specific action plans. For instance, instead of saying, "This always happens," reframe the situation by asking, "What can I do differently?"

- Convert criticism of others into opportunities for collaboration and understanding.

- Shift focus from what is delayed or broken to what can be accomplished right now.

- Create new patterns of thinking by asking, "What else is possible?" in challenging situations.

- Use setbacks as prompts to explore unexpected alternatives and creative solutions.

4. Possibilities

Imagine standing at a crossroads. One path leads down the familiar trail of blaming market conditions and the economy and complaining about costs—dark, well-worn, and ultimately circular. The other opens to a landscape of possibility. The difference between staying stuck and step-ping into that new territory comes down to three powerful elements: awareness, choice, and transformation. Together, the ACT Formula can guide you from negativity to possibility.

This formula isn't magic; it is a methodology—practical pathway from blaming and complaining into a world of possibility. Every moment of awareness is an invitation to choice. Every choice is an opportunity to transform. And every transformation moves you further along the path from negativity to possibility.

You don't have to like your circumstances to transform them. You don't need to deny problems exist. You simply need to shift your energy from what you can't control to what you can. This isn't about forcing positivity; it's about choosing productivity. When you catch yourself blaming or complaining, ask: "What problem am I actually trying to solve here?" And, "Is this the most effective way to solve it?"

Moving Forward

As my agency story showed, eliminating stress and creating success emerge not from perfect circumstances but from how we respond to imperfect ones. Each time you catch yourself blaming or complaining, remember what Charlie accomplished when he had us focus our energy. He didn't deny the problems—those were undeniable—but instead chose to focus on solutions instead of blaming and complaining.

KEY TAKEAWAYS

- If you want to get ahead in life, there are two things you must give up: blaming and complaining. *No blaming, no complaining, and no excuses* is a sign I have in my G'Raj Mahal (a really amazing man cave) to remind me daily that this is the way.

- Blaming and complaining drain the energy needed for happiness and growth. Instead, focus on solutions.

- The ACT Formula provides a practical path forward: Awareness + Choice + Transform = Possibilities.

- Small shifts in focus create major life transformations.

- Your position in the Insight–Implementation Matrix can change through practice. The four categories are: the Pioneer, the Observer, the Reactor, and the Defender.

REFLECTION QUESTIONS

1. Which Matrix quadrant do you typically operate in?

....

....

....

....

2. What do you complain about most often? Who or what do you blame?

....

....

....

3. Where could using the ACT Formula create immediate change?

....

....

....

....

4. What one situation would transform with a different focus?

....

....

....

....

ACTION STEPS

1. **Track Your Patterns**
   - Note blame triggers for one week and write them down.
   - Document complaint habits.
   - Identify pivot opportunities.

....

....

....

....

....

2. Practice One Pivot

- Choose your most common complaint.
- Create three possible solutions and pick one.
- Test it for three days.

....

....

....

....

3. Build Support

- Share your commitment with someone.
- Schedule weekly check-ins.
- Document your progress.

....

....

....

....

LOOKING AHEAD

In the next chapter, we will explore the Blame Loop—the self-reinforcing cycle that keeps us stuck—and begin understanding how to break free. But for now, take a moment to consider what might become possible if you could see what you are currently missing.

The issue is not that you are solving problems incorrectly. It is that *you are solving the wrong problems perfectly*. Solving the correct problems begins with recognizing when you might be blind to what matters most.

WHEN YOU BLAME AND
CRITICIZE OTHERS, YOU
ARE AVOIDING SOME TRUTH
ABOUT YOURSELF.

—**Deepak Chopra, bestselling author**

CHAPTER 3

The Blame Loop Revealed

THE BLAME LOOP™ IS A PSYCHOLOGICAL ROUNDABOUT where every exit seems to lead back to the entrance. This loop is not just a cycle of failure; it is a masterfully disguised trap that keeps us investing time, energy, and hope into solving the wrong problems. Like a skilled magician's illusion, the Blame Loop directs our attention away from what matters, leaving us frustrated, confused, and increasingly desperate for answers.

Imagine trying to fix a car's engine by repeatedly washing its exterior. No matter how thoroughly or how hard you scrub, or which premium cleaning products you use, the engine problem persists, worsening and ultimately destroying the car. That's what the Blame Loop does to our lives. It has us furiously solving the wrong problems while the real issues remain untouched, under the hood, invisible to our desperate efforts. In this cycle we not only fail to find solutions; we become physiologically incapable of seeing the actual problem.

The most insidious part? Every cycle through the Blame Loop strengthens its hold on us. Each attempt to break free using our familiar thinking patterns only tightens the Blame Loop's grip. It's like running on a hamster wheel: The faster you run with your usual approach, the more energy you waste going nowhere.

But the truth changes everything. Understanding the Blame Loop serves as a map of the prison you've been living in, drawn by those who have studied thousands of people stuck in the same patterns. And once you can understand the layout of the prison, you can plot your escape.

In this chapter, we'll dissect the five elements of the Blame Loop, each a critical piece of the puzzle that keeps us trapped. More importantly, we'll learn why simply trying harder, being more disciplined, or "staying positive" is not enough. The journey out of the Loop begins with a crucial concept that I mentioned at the end of the last chapter.

You are not failing at solving your problems.
You are succeeding at solving the wrong problems perfectly.

Mia stood in front of her bathroom mirror, tears streaming down her face: another failed diet, another morning of self-loathing. "I just don't have enough willpower. I'll start again tomorrow," she whispered to her reflection. This wasn't the first time Mia felt this way. She had thrown herself into grueling, almost insane workouts—two-hour gym sessions, endless cardio, and strict meal plans—only to find herself frustrated when the scale refused to budge. Mia didn't realize that she wasn't just looking at herself. She was staring directly into the Blame Loop, an invisible prison that shapes our reality, colors every experience, and defines how we see ourselves and the world around us.

Have you ever felt trapped like Mia? Perhaps it wasn't about diet or willpower. Maybe it was watching another relationship crumble for the same reasons as the last one, or staring at yet another resignation letter, convinced that this time you've finally found the right company to jump to. You're not alone. Millions of us walk in circles in a dark room, convinced we're making progress simply because we're moving. We tell ourselves stories about why things aren't working, each one more convincing than the last:

- *I'm just not disciplined enough.*
- *Nobody understands what I'm trying to do.*

- *The timing isn't right. I'll try again when things settle down.*
- *I'm not succeeding because of this toxic work environment. I need to find a better company.*
- *If I could get out of this relationship, everything would be different.*
- *I won't become one of those people. Success would change who I am.*

That last one is particularly sneaky. We often look at successful people and tell ourselves, "That guy is a jerk and a loser" (even though you've never spoken to him). "Successful people are all greedy," or "They've lost touch with reality," or "They've sacrificed everything that matters."

We build our identity around not being like them, self-sabotaging without even knowing what we're doing, turning our stagnation into a badge of authenticity. These aren't just excuses; they are comfortable lies we have polished into truths, each feeling more genuine than the last. They are the stories we tell ourselves at three o'clock in the morning, the justifications that feel so right they must be real. But no, they are only sophisticated prison bars, invisible yet stronger than steel, keeping us trapped in the same patterns while convincing us we are making progress.

- "You just need more discipline," your trainer says, carefully repeating your goals back to you. What you hear beneath the words: *You are lazy. You lack willpower. You're a quitter.*

- "You need to be more proactive," your boss suggests during your performance review. The unspoken message lands hard: *You're always behind. You can't plan ahead. You are not leadership material.*

- "Maybe you're just not trying the right approach," your mother offers with her familiar concerned tone. The implied criticism stings: *You are doing it wrong—again. Like always.*

- "You just need to push yourself harder," your father repeats, as he has since you were young. Behind his words, you make the same painful assumption: *I am not enough. I will never be enough.*

These well-intentioned messages, wrapped in the guise of support, reinforce our deepest self-doubts and keep us locked in cycles of blame. They are the echoes of others' limitations projected onto our struggles, and they have no place in our path forward. Though wrapped in good intentions, each piece of advice pushes you further into the maze of self-blame. These people are not bad. They are simply viewing your struggles through the distorted lens of their Blame Loops, offering solutions that worked superficially for them while missing the deeper patterns at play.

FIVE COMPONENTS OF THE BLAME LOOP

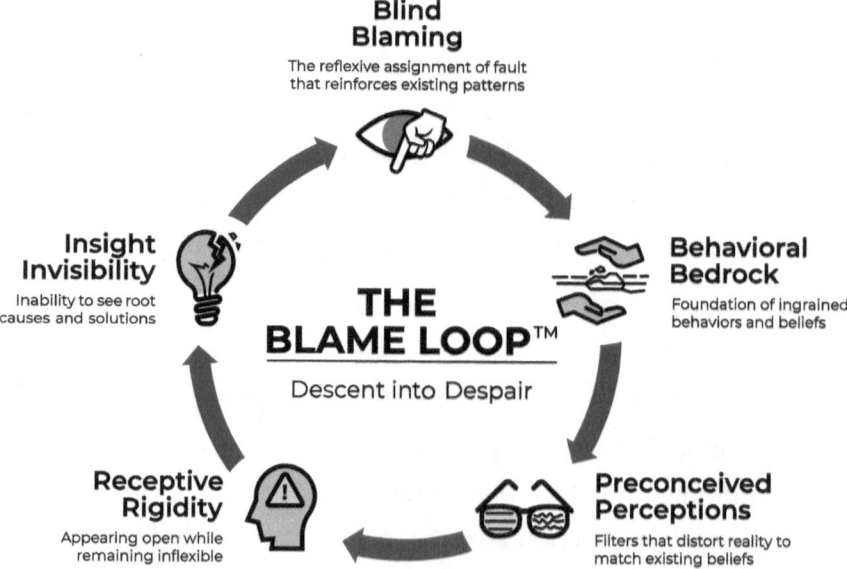

The circular diagram of the Blame Loop is like a psychological merry-go-round, and each segment represents a crucial component that keeps the whole machine spinning. These aren't just parts working in isolation; they are interconnected pieces of a masterfully engineered system designed to keep us dizzy and disoriented and somehow always end up where we started.

The **Behavioral Bedrock** component is the platform we're standing on—seemingly solid but constantly in motion. As we spin, the **Preconceived Perceptions** component acts like warped mirrors, distorting everything we see outside our rotating prison. The **Receptive Rigidity** component functions as the centrifugal force, holding us firmly in place while we insist we can step off any time we want. **Insight Invisibility** has a dizzying effect on our vision, turning clear paths to freedom into smeared streaks of light we can no longer trust or follow. Finally, the **Blind Blaming** component becomes the motor that powers the whole machine, and many times, our sphere of influence (friends, family, bosses, colleagues) grabs the bars as well, providing the momentum that keeps us spinning, making every attempt to step off feel dangerous and wrong.

With each rotation, the ride spins faster, the vertigo intensifies, and our grip on reality becomes more tenuous. Like a carnival ride gone wrong, what started as mild discomfort transforms into gut-churning disorientation. The faster we spin, the sicker we feel, yet the dizziness convinces us that stopping would be even worse. We close our eyes, hold on tighter, and tell ourselves this is normal—that everyone else must feel this way too. The nausea of perpetual spinning becomes our new normal.

The arrows connecting each component in our diagram aren't just decorative lines—the mechanical gears linking each part to the next. When one component activates, the others must follow. Like any well-engineered system, each component reinforces the others, creating a self-perpetuating cycle that becomes smoother and more powerful with each nauseating rotation.

Let's examine each component of this hypnotic machinery that is deeply woven into our being to understand how these parts work together to keep us spinning when we think we're moving forward, and why simply hoping the dizziness will pass isn't enough to break free.

BEHAVIORAL BEDROCK:
THE FOUNDATION OF FAILURE

Every house needs a foundation, but what happens when that foundation is engineered for failure? Our minds work like architects who have learned the wrong lessons so completely that they can't help but recreate the same flawed blueprints over and over. In his groundbreaking work *Thinking, Fast and Slow*, Daniel Kahneman revealed a startling truth: Our brains are master architects of shortcuts and snap judgments, building neural highways that become our default paths through life—paths paved with good intentions but often leading to predictable failures.[1]

Your Behavioral Bedrock isn't just the foundation of your mental house; it's the ground beneath it. Like geological layers formed over time, it has been shaped and compressed by:

- Early life experiences that carved deep grooves in your thinking
- Cultural conditioning that whispers constant judgments
- Past successes that became future traps
- Deep-seated beliefs about how the world "should" work

This bedrock feels solid, unquestionable, and true. After all, how can you question the very ground you're standing on? But here's the cruel irony: The more solid this foundation feels, the more likely it is to crack under the weight of reality. It's a foundation built to fail, designed with fatal flaws we can't see because we are standing on them.

Ava, a brilliant executive I counseled, needed help understanding why her team was underperforming. Her Behavioral Bedrock was built in the trenches of her early career, where a demanding boss taught her that "pressure creates diamonds." Twenty years later, she was still applying pressure, watching her diamonds crumble into dust—a perfect example of what Stephen Covey would call a paradigm in desperate need of shifting.[2]

PRECONCEIVED PERCEPTIONS: THE FILTERS THAT FAIL US

If Behavioral Bedrock forms the foundation of our thinking, Preconceived Perceptions are the filters through which we view the world. But these aren't just simple screens. They are sophisticated distortion machines that process reality into what we're willing to see while filtering out anything that challenges our existing beliefs. Like a sophisticated security system gone wrong, these filters work tirelessly to "protect" us from the truths that could set us free.

To understand the devastating power of these failed filters, consider one of the most tragic examples in medical history: the story of Ignaz Semmelweis, a Hungarian physician in the 1840s. Semmelweis made a discovery that should have been immediately obvious and embraced. He observed that in his hospital, physicians routinely moved between performing autopsies and delivering babies without washing their hands. In contrast, midwives, who did not perform autopsies, had significantly lower mortality rates among their patients in the maternity ward. When Semmelweis implemented mandatory hand-washing protocols for physicians before they attended to births, the results were dramatic: The mortality rate in his division plummeted from 18 percent to less than 2 percent.[3]

This wasn't just a minor improvement. It was the difference between life and death for countless mothers. The evidence was clear, consistent, and overwhelming. Semmelweis had discovered a way to save thousands of lives with nothing more than chemicals, soap, and water. Yet this life-saving truth couldn't pass the medical establishment's perceptual filters.

Respected doctors not only rejected his findings but ridiculed them. These intelligent men, trained in the scientific method, looked at clear statistical evidence of saved lives, but their filters transformed it into nonsense. Their Preconceived Perceptions had become an anti-vision system, actively blocking life-saving information from reaching their understanding.

Why would educated professionals filter out such obvious evidence? Their preconceived notions about the disease—that it was caused by "bad air" or an imbalance of humor—weren't just ideas. They were automated filtering systems, processing every piece of information through a complex network of existing beliefs. Evidence that didn't fit their paradigm was not only rejected, it was filtered out before it could even reach conscious consideration.

The most chilling part is that these doctors believed their filters worked perfectly. Each time they dismissed Semmelweis's evidence, they felt they were maintaining high medical standards. Their preconceived perceptions created what Peter Senge, founding chairperson of the Society for Organizational Learning, senior lecturer at MIT, and author of *The Fifth Discipline*, would later call "mental models"—deeply ingrained filters that shape how we see the world and convince us we see it with perfect clarity.[4]

Semmelweis was eventually driven out of medicine, his reputation shredded by the filters he was trying to clean. He died in an asylum, his mind broken by the weight of watching mothers die needlessly while doctors, convinced of their clear vision, literally walked from autopsy rooms to delivery wards with unwashed hands. It would take decades for germ theory to be accepted and hand washing to become standard medical practice. How many died in those intervening years? How many lives were sacrificed because of filters that failed their most basic task of revealing the truth?

This isn't just a historical tragedy. As Marshall McLuhan, a Canadian philosopher, noted, "We don't know who discovered water, but we know it wasn't a fish."[5] Our perceptual filters are just as invisible to us as water is to fish, just as invisible as germs were to nineteenth-century doctors.

They silently process our reality, automatically sorting information into "acceptable" and "impossible" without conscious awareness.

We need to break free from these filters. But how do you destroy a filter you can't see? As Einstein famously noted, "We cannot solve our problems with the same thinking we used when we created them."[6] What is the most dangerous aspect of these failed filters? They don't feel like filters. Instead, they feel like crystal-clear windows onto reality. It is no different than me standing in the batter's box during baseball practice, unable to connect with the ball no matter how hard I tried. I thought I had a clear view of the pitch, but my vision was blurry. I just didn't know it.

As those nineteenth-century doctors thought they were seeing clearly, we can also get a distorted view of truth. But what vital evidence are our filters blocking? What life-changing insights are we automatically discarding? What obvious solutions remain invisible because our filters have labeled them "impossible"? Just like I couldn't hit the ball until I corrected my vision, we can't solve problems we don't realize we are not seeing clearly. Recognizing and challenging our filters is like putting on those glasses. It's the first step toward seeing the world as it is.

As we will see in the next component of the Blame Loop, these failed filters lead us directly into an even more devious trap called Receptive Rigidity, where our minds become as inflexible as they are convinced of their clarity.

RECEPTIVE RIGIDITY:
THE PRISON WE PRAISE

"I'm always open to feedback," Rachel told me during a coaching session, her voice carrying the confident tone of someone who truly believed what she was saying. Within minutes, however, she systematically dismantled every suggestion I made about what needed to be improved in her business. Each insight I offered was met with a perfectly rational explanation of why I was wrong and how that wouldn't work in her area. Rachel wasn't just defending her position. She was demonstrating what Harvard professor Chris Argyris called "defensive reasoning," a sophisticated form of self-deception where we protect ourselves from the truths that could set us free. A mental model designed to maintain a sense of control and avoid appearing flawed.[7]

Welcome to Receptive Rigidity, the most cunningly disguised component of the Blame Loop. Like a prison with mirrors for walls, it creates the illusion of openness while keeping us firmly confined within our existing beliefs. The true genius of this prison is that we not only accept it; we praise it as wisdom.

Consider Nokia, once the undisputed king of mobile phones. After brilliantly disrupting Motorola's dominance in the industry, Nokia achieved what seemed impossible: capturing nearly 50 percent of the global mobile phone market. They were innovative, adaptable, and proud of their ability to understand changing consumer needs. When their engineers suggested developing smartphones with large touchscreens, Nokia's leadership confidently listened to all perspectives—and then explained why such devices would never catch on.

"We know what our customers want," they declared, even as the iPhone began reshaping the industry. "We're open to innovation, but it has to make sense," they insisted, as Samsung started gaining ground. Nokia's leaders weren't ignoring reality. They were actively engaging with it, discussing it, analyzing it, and fitting it neatly into their existing paradigm. By the time they realized their error, their market share had plummeted to single digits.

This pattern isn't unique to Nokia. Kodak, another industry titan, invented the digital camera, proudly displaying its receptiveness to new technology. Then, trapped in its prison of "openness," the company explained precisely why digital photography would never replace film—right up until it did, pushing the company into bankruptcy.

In *The Innovator's Dilemma*, Clayton Christensen revealed why this happens: Receptive Rigidity isn't about ignoring new ideas; it's about engaging with them in a way that renders them harmless to our existing beliefs. We don't dismiss innovation; we suffocate it with rational analysis based on past success.[8]

The most cunning aspect of this prison is that the stronger its walls become, the more we praise our openness. We become so convinced of our receptivity that we can't see our rigidity. It's like a judge declaring, "I've heard all the evidence," while wearing noise-canceling headphones. We don't just reject new ideas. We actively engage with them, analyze them, and then explain precisely why they don't apply to our situation. Think of it like a museum curator who is proud of acquiring new artifacts, only to immediately classify each according to existing categories, never considering that the categories might need updating. The curator isn't ignoring new acquisitions. He is actively processing them in a way that preserves the existing order.

Einstein's famous observation—"Insanity is doing the same thing repeatedly and expecting different results"—takes on new meaning here. The true insanity isn't in the repetition; it's in our sophisticated rationalization of why this time will be different, all while praising our openness to change.

As we move to the next component of the Blame Loop, Insight Invisibility, we will see how this prison of praise sets us up for an even more profound form of blindness—one in which solutions become invisible to us, no matter how they present themselves.

INSIGHT INVISIBILITY: THE BLINDNESS WE CAN'T SEE

Have you ever watched a magician make something disappear? The object is right there one moment and gone the next. The trick works because your mind fills in the gaps, creating a reality where the vanished object simply ceases to exist. Insight Invisibility works the same way. Except in this case, the magician is your mind, and what vanishes are not coins or cards but solutions that could transform your life or business.

The story of Blockbuster versus Netflix perfectly illustrates this psychological vanishing act. In 2000, Blockbuster had the opportunity to purchase Netflix for $50 million—a chance to own the future of entertainment delivery. The Netflix team laid out their vision: Streaming technology would transform how people consume content, and the video rental industry needed to evolve. The solution to Blockbuster's future challenges was available and sitting directly across them at the negotiating table.

But something remarkable happened: The solution didn't just get rejected; it became invisible. This wasn't simple short-sightedness. The Blockbuster team wasn't stupid or lazy. They were experiencing what Joel Barker, author and futurist, calls "paradigm paralysis," where solutions vanish because they don't fit our existing framework of understanding.[9] Like someone trying to read a book in a language they don't know, Blockbuster's leaders were staring directly at the future of their industry but had lost the ability to comprehend what they were seeing.

"The store experience is what customers want," they insisted, even as Netflix's membership grew. "People enjoy browsing the aisles," they maintained as streaming technology advanced. "Late fees are a necessary part of the business model," they declared, even as Netflix eliminated them. These statements weren't just wrong; they were evidence of solutions becoming invisible in real-time.

They had all the puzzle pieces necessary for success but were unable to see the picture they could create. Blockbuster saw each component—the technology, the changing consumer preferences, the rising competition. Still, the corporate minds at Blockbuster had filtered out the connecting patterns, leaving them unable to assemble a coherent picture that demanded action.

Our brains are wired to see what we expect to see and to make any-thing that doesn't fit vanish from awareness. It's not that we actively reject solutions. They simply don't register in our consciousness. As philosopher Immanuel Kant realized centuries ago, we don't just observe reality; we actively construct it through the categories of our understanding.[10] When something falls outside those categories, our minds perform the ultimate magic trick: making it invisible while also making us forget it was ever there. The most dangerous aspect of Insight Invisibility is our complete inability to perceive that something might be missing. It's like a magic show where we've forgotten we're watching magic, convinced that disap-pearing acts are just how reality works.

Think about your own life. What solutions might your mind be making vanish right now? What opportunities are sitting across your metaphorical negotiating table, as clear as Netflix was to Blockbuster, yet somehow remain invisible to you? What books are you trying to read in a language your paradigms won't let you understand? Are you suffering from Insight Invisibility right now?

As we move to the final component of the Blame Loop, Blind Blaming, we'll see how the inability to see solutions sets us up for the most destructive phase—where we assign fault based on a reality our minds have already altered beyond recognition.

BLIND BLAMING: THE KEYSTONE OF CHAOS

Look at any stone arch that has stood for centuries, and you'll find one crucial element that makes it all possible: the keystone. This wedge-shaped stone at the arch's apex doesn't just sit there. It actively transfers the weight and pressure from above, directing forces outward and down through the arch's curve. Remove the keystone, and the entire structure collapses.

This is why Blind Blaming is so important to thoroughly understand.

It is the keystone that holds the entire psychological arch in place, reinforcing each component we've discussed:

- It strengthens our Behavioral Bedrock by providing evidence for our beliefs.

- It validates our Preconceived Perceptions by finding what we expect to find.

- It reinforces our Receptive Rigidity by proving we were right all along.

- It deepens our Insight Invisibility by directing attention away from real solutions.

There is an opportunity hidden within this structure: Remove the keystone, and the arch will not stand. This book focuses on Blind Blaming, the leverage point that can bring down the whole system of failure. It is a sophisticated system of misdirection. When you engage in Blind Blaming, you are not merely assigning fault but actively reinforcing your inability to see reality clearly.

When facing challenges, we instinctively deflect responsibility by crafting convenient narratives. We blame our past, lamenting, "I never learned the right skills in school." We hide behind our self-imposed identity, claiming, "I am too creative to be good with details." And when confronted with criticism, we dismiss valuable feedback by thinking, *This person has no idea how hard I work and what I've given up for this company!*

These surface-level excuses are just the beginning. As we dig deeper, our blame becomes more entrenched and personal. We let our background define our future: "Growing up poor means I will never understand money." We turn personality traits into insurmountable barriers: "I am too introverted to be a good leader." When challenged, we respond with defensive counterattacks: "If you had my responsibilities, you'd be stressed too." All the while, real solutions remain obscured behind these carefully constructed barriers.

But perhaps most dangerous are the sophisticated forms of blame that masquerade as wisdom or virtue. We convince ourselves we're acting nobly: "I'm protecting my team by not delegating." We wrap our resistance in the language of authenticity: "Being authentic means I can't play the corporate game." We reframe our defensiveness as passion: "Getting defensive just shows how passionate I am about my work." We blame our environment: "This city doesn't have the right opportunities." And we transform legitimate criticism into attacks on our authority: "When people question my decisions, they undermine my authority."

Each of these statements or beliefs sound insightful, even self-aware, which is what makes them so dangerous—blame disguised as wisdom; reactions masked as responses. This pattern becomes particularly dangerous because it spreads. Like a virus of misunderstanding, Blind Blaming infects our relationships, our teams, and our organizations. Family members, colleagues, and even entire companies can become caught in the same loop, each person's Blind Blaming reinforcing and validating everyone else's.

Think of it as a game of hot potato with responsibility, except no one can see the potato. We reflexively and instinctively toss blame around, each throw reinforcing the very structures that keep us trapped. We blame what seems obvious because our keystone has made anything else invisible. But here's the revolutionary insight: When you understand and address Blind Blaming, you won't have to dismantle each component of the Blame Loop individually. Like removing a keystone, addressing this one element can cause the entire structure to shift, creating space for new understanding and real solutions to emerge.

We've spent an entire chapter exploring the depths of Blind Blaming because it's a problem that makes all other problems unsolvable. It's the keystone that turns five separate components into a self-reinforcing prison of perception. As we move forward, remember that the goal isn't to shore up this arch; it's to remove its keystone. Only then can we break free from the Blame Loop and begin to see our challenges as they are, not as our blame-distorted vision has made them appear.

THE VICIOUS CYCLE: WHY IS IT SO HARD TO BREAK FREE?

Trapped in the Loop

The more times we cycle through the Blame Loop, the more it becomes like psychological bedrock—layers of beliefs compressed over time until they seem as solid as stone. Like geological strata telling the story of Earth's past, these layers of accumulated patterns tell the story of our limitations. Our thinking becomes fossilized, our perceptions calcified, each rotation adding another layer of sediment that hardens into seemingly unchangeable truth. We mistake these accumulated layers for foundational reality, forgetting that even bedrock can be transformed with enough pressure and time.

Breaking Free

Understanding the Blame Loop isn't just about recognizing patterns; it's about finding the fault lines in our psychological bedrock where transformation becomes possible. Real breakthroughs don't come from adding more layers to our existing paradigms.

I've been fortunate to teach all over the world for twenty-five years, and I've found most people have heard the common phrase "paradigm shift" or "paradigm," but they don't know what it really means. And yes, I know someone is thinking, *No, a paradigm is* not *two dimes.*

A paradigm is a set of rules or a framework of thinking that defines how we approach and solve problems within a specific context. A paradigm shift occurs when we create enough pressure to crack through our accumulated layers of belief, fundamentally changing how we perceive and address issues. Essentially, it's a complete transformation of our mental landscape.

In his book *Paradigms*, Joel Barker describes a paradigm as "any set of rules or regulations that describes boundaries and tells us how to be successful within those boundaries."[11] This idea of questioning paradigms becomes critical to creating the pressure needed for real transformation.

Breaking free requires something more profound and challenging than adding new layers to old thinking. Like tectonic forces that reshape entire landscapes, true change comes from pressures applied at the right points, in the right ways. The solutions we need often lie outside our crystallized patterns—visible only when we are willing to break through our comfortable strata of thinking.

KEY TAKEAWAYS

The Blame Loop: Five Components

- Behavioral Bedrock forms our foundation of beliefs.
- Preconceived Perceptions filter our reality.
- Receptive Rigidity makes us inflexible while believing we are open.
- Insight Invisibility blinds us to solutions.
- Blind Blaming acts as the keystone holding the entire system in place.

The Reinforcing Nature: Each trip through the Loop doesn't just repeat the cycle. It strengthens it, adding layers of calcified thinking that make breaking free increasingly difficult.

The Keystone Effect: Understanding Blind Blaming as the keystone offers hope. Remove this one component, and the entire structure can begin to shift.

REFLECTION QUESTIONS _____

1. Component Recognition:

- Which component of the Blame Loop resonates most strongly with your experience(s)?

....

....

- Where do you see these patterns playing out in your life?

....

....

- Which component seems most active in your professional life? Your personal life?

....

....

2. Pattern Awareness:

- How has the Blame Loop been reinforcing itself in your life?

....

....

- What solutions might you be making invisible?

....

....

- Where might you be praising your prison?

....

....

....

3. **Resistance Check**:
   - After reading this chapter, which concepts did you find yourself resisting?

   ....

   ....

   - What explanations or justifications came to mind?

   ....

   ....

   - Where did you find yourself thinking, *Yes, but . . . ?*

   ....

   ....

ACTION STEPS

1. **Map Your Blame Loop**
   - Choose one recurring challenge in your life.
   - Identify how each component of the Blame Loop operates in this situation.
   - Pay special attention to what or who you might be blaming.

   ....

   ....

   ....

   ....

   ....

2. Track Your Reactions

- For the next week, notice when you feel defensive.
- Write down your immediate reactions to challenges.
- Look for patterns in your blame responses.

....

....

....

....

3. Challenge Your Certainty

- List three things you are certain about in your field.
- Question why you feel so confident about them.
- Consider what might happen if they were not true.

....

....

....

....

4. Share and Validate

- Discuss your Blame Loop observations with someone you trust.
- Ask them where they see these patterns in their own life.
- Notice any resistance that comes up during the conversation.

LOOKING AHEAD

You've now mapped the intricate patterns of your Blame Loop. You've seen how each blame-shifting cycle reinforces itself, how each iteration deepens the grooves of your habitual responses, and—most important-ly—why your previous attempts at change may have only strengthened these self-defeating patterns.

In the next chapter, we will begin to explore the first of three simple steps in a powerful framework that can help you break free from this cycle. The solution is simple but will challenge everything your Blame Loop has convinced you is unchangeable truth.

Are you ready to break through?

PART TWO

THE RCD METHOD™

THE WISE MAN QUESTIONS
HIMSELF, THE FOOL OTHERS.

—Henri Arnol, cartoonist

CHAPTER 4

Reflect: Discover the Hidden Truth

———

WHEN SOMETHING IS HOLDING YOU BACK, the real obstacle often isn't what you think it is. That's why traditional problem-solving approaches fail us time and time again. We get caught in the Blame Loop, pointing fingers at surface-level issues, while the real cause remains hidden. To break free from this cycle, we need a fundamentally different approach.

Enter the **RCD Method**™, a revolutionary three-step process for uncovering and overcoming what is really holding you back:

THE RCD METHOD ™

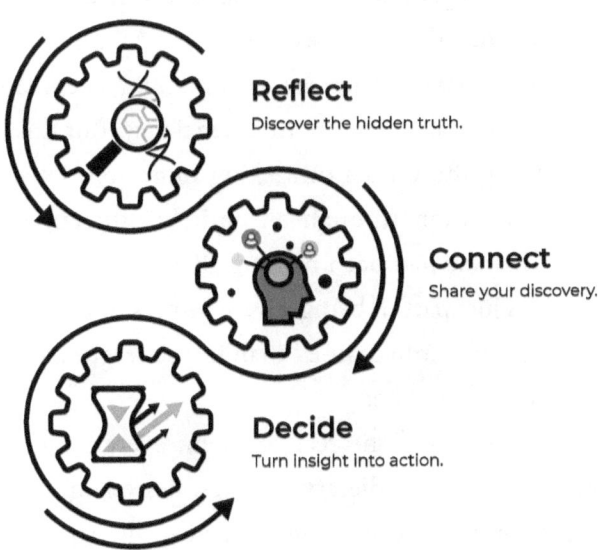

Reflect
Discover the hidden truth.

Connect
Share your discovery.

Decide
Turn insight into action.

1. **Reflect**: Discover the hidden truth.
2. **Connect**: Share your discovery.
3. **Decide**: Turn insight into action.

Instead of asking, "What is the problem?" or "Who is to blame?" the RCD Method starts with a more powerful question: "Is there something else going on?" This simple shift—from looking for problems to discovering hidden truths—changes everything. In the next three chapters, we will explore each step of the RCD Method in detail, beginning with Reflect, where we'll learn to uncover the real obstacles that have been hiding behind our sophisticated excuses.

WHAT HAVE YOU BEEN MISSING?

Sophia sat in the doctor's office, staring at her latest blood test results. Everything looked "normal," yet she felt anything but normal. Chronic fatigue dragged at her bones, her relationships were suffering, and despite working harder than ever, she felt stuck in every area of her life. Like most of us, Sophia had tried all the obvious solutions: new diets, exercise programs, meditation apps, relationship books, career counseling, and time management systems. Each "fix" seemed to make things worse, like taking aspirin for a broken leg—temporary relief masking deepening damage.

The real issue revealed a severe iron deficiency. But this discovery was not about running more tests or seeking more solutions. It was about looking at her situation through an entirely different lens—one that would reveal what she had been missing all along. Sophia had dismissed her exhaustion as just part of being a busy professional, never questioning why she felt so much more drained than her colleagues, or why her usual resilience had abandoned her.

Once she understood the real problem, everything changed. With iron supplementation and dietary changes, her energy began to return. But the bigger transformation came from what this experience taught her about listening to her body and questioning her assumptions. "I used to pride myself on pushing through anything," Sophia reflected. "But I've learned that sometimes what we dismiss as 'normal' is our body's way of signaling that something deeper needs attention. Instead of adding another productivity app or workout class to my schedule, I needed to stop and ask myself: *What is my body trying to tell me?* That simple shift in perspective changed everything."

OBSTACLES VS. PROBLEMS: WORDS MATTER

Picture the last time you felt genuinely stuck. Maybe it was a business challenge that wouldn't budge, a health goal that kept slipping away, or a relationship pattern you couldn't break. If you are like most people, you probably called it a "problem" and tried to solve it repeatedly by using the same thinking that created it in the first place.

But what if the way we think about our challenges is itself part of the challenge? What if labeling something a "problem" makes it harder to overcome? I learned this lesson firsthand during a difficult libel and slander case I recently won. When my attorney said, "Kevin, words matter," it wasn't just about legal terminology; it was about how the language we choose shapes our entire approach to challenges.

Initially, I saw the situation as an insurmountable problem: people saying untrue things about me, a permanent stain on my reputation. But everything changed when I shifted my perspective to see it as an obstacle to navigate rather than a problem to be stuck with.

Yes, it left a scar, but it also taught me that how we label our challenges determines how we handle them. Just as I learned to approach the legal situation strategically rather than simply enduring it, we can all choose more empowering language when facing difficulties. Consider the difference between a problem and an obstacle. A problem feels permanent—something to be endured or solved through sheer force of will.

Conversely, an obstacle can be navigated by being crossed, circumvented, or even transformed into an advantage. This shift in language isn't just semantic. It is transformative. When we reframe our challenges as obstacles, new possibilities emerge. A problem might feel overwhelming, but an obstacle invites strategy, creativity, and adaptability. Problems feel heavy and unmovable, but obstacles invite action. This subtle shift in perspective can transform how you approach challenges, turning stagnation into movement. From this point forward, we'll make a critical shift in our language and thinking. We're not dealing with problems anymore; we're facing obstacles.

THE POWER OF O-DNA: YOUR DISCOVERY FRAMEWORK

O-DNA (Obstacle Deep Nexus Analysis) is like a powerful flashlight in a dark room. You know something important is there, but you've been searching in the wrong places or getting distracted by shadows. O-DNA helps you systematically illuminate every corner until you find that one crucial thing you've been missing.

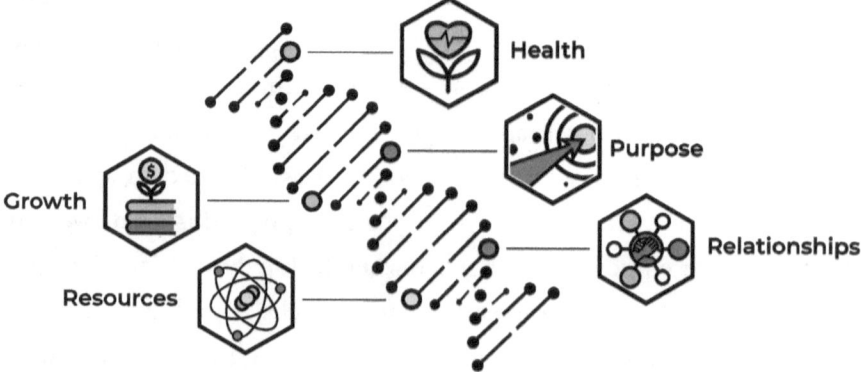

Obstacle Deep Nexus Analysis (O-DNA)

When you'are **HEALTHY** and clear on your **PURPOSE**, committed to **GROWTH**, supported by strong **RELATIONSHIPS**, and equipped with the right **RESOURCES**, you can overcome any obstacle.

Health

Purpose

Relationships

Growth

Resources

This discovery framework examines five core areas, or "strands," where your root cause might be hiding. But here's the key: You're not trying to fix all five areas. You're using them as lenses to find that one thing that has been hiding in plain sight—the real root cause that, once addressed, will create a ripple effect of positive change across your entire life.

Let's explore each strand with the kind of deep, honest questioning that reveals hidden truths.

THE HEALTH STRAND: YOUR FOUNDATION FOR EVERYTHING

Your health isn't just about feeling good or bad. It's the foundation that supports every other aspect of your life. Often, what we dismiss as "just getting older" or "normal stress" could be the key to understanding our deeper obstacles.

Simon was what most people would consider "successful." As the CEO of a rapidly growing tech company, he had everything he thought he wanted—influence, respect, and a seven-figure income. But lately, his performance was slipping. His decision-making felt clouded, his patience was paper-thin, and his leadership team had started tiptoeing around his volatile moods.

At first, he blamed the pressure of scaling the company. Then he pointed to difficult market conditions, challenging employees, and endless demands on his time. But when he examined his Health Strand, he discovered something deeper: He had been treating his body like a machine that could run indefinitely without maintenance. Years of getting only five hours of sleep at night, skipped meals replaced by coffee, and a sedentary lifestyle weren't just affecting his health—they were undermining every aspect of his leadership and life.

Start with asking yourself questions in these five critical categories:

1. **Physical Activity**: Do you work out at least forty-five minutes a day? This isn't about intense gym sessions. It's about consistent, daily movement. Many obstacles we face in business and life stem from a stagnant body trying to support an active mind.

2. **Medical Oversight**: Do you go to the doctor for regular check-ups? Not just when something is wrong, but for preventive care. The root cause of your current challenge might be hiding in basic health markers you have neglected.

3. **Hormone Health**: Do you have bloodwork drawn regularly that includes hormone checks? Hormones affect everything from energy and mood to decision-making and relationship dynamics. Many people struggle for years with issues that could be resolved through proper hormone monitoring and balance.

4. **Nutrition Strategy**: Do you follow a nutrition plan? Not a diet, but a structured approach to fueling your body. What looks like a motivation problem might actually be a nutrition issue.

5. **Sleep Quality**: Do you get at least seven or eight hours of quality sleep each night? Poor sleep often lurks beneath the surface of many daily challenges—from lack of focus and diminished creativity to mood swings and reduced decision-making ability. Many attribute these issues to stress or workload when the root cause is actually disrupted sleep patterns. This can stem from common but overlooked habits like late-night screen time, irregular sleep schedules, or undiagnosed conditions like sleep apnea. Quality sleep isn't a luxury; it is a fundamental pillar that supports every aspect of our physical and mental performance.

When exploring the Health Strand, look for:

- Tests or assessments you have been postponing
- Symptoms you have been normalizing
- Changes you have been attributing to age or stress

- The inability to start working out . . . today
- Connections between physical symptoms and life challenges

Document everything, especially the things that seem unrelated to your current obstacle. Sometimes the most important clues come from connections we initially dismiss as irrelevant. When Simon finally prioritized his health, everything changed. He started with one simple commitment: seven hours of sleep, nonnegotiable. He stopped watching TV and checking his phone in bed, replacing digital distractions with physical books before sleep. He even started charging his phone by his treadmill each night, forcing himself to go to the treadmill to get his "precious" device in the morning, making it easier to start his daily movement routine.

Within weeks, his mood stabilized, his decisions improved, and his team noticed the difference. He then gradually added morning workouts and a structured nutrition plan. Six months later, he wasn't just a better leader—he was a different person. His company's performance improved not because he worked more, but because he finally built the physical foundation to support his ambitions. His energy, clarity, and resilience transformed business results, his relationships at home, and his sense of daily fulfillment.

THE PURPOSE STRAND: YOUR INNER COMPASS

Your purpose isn't just about having lofty goals or an inspiring mission statement. It is the internal compass that gives meaning to every decision you make. Often, what we dismiss as "burnout" or "success fatigue" is actually a signal that we have lost connection with our deeper why.

Elena had built what most people would call a dream life. She ran a successful million-dollar-a-year business, had a beautiful home, and was surrounded by people who admired her. But deep down, something wasn't right. She felt restless, unfulfilled, and oddly disconnected—from her work, her relationships, even from herself.

At first, she blamed stress, then burnout, then the constant pressure of running a business. But when she examined her Purpose Strand, she realized the real issue: She had no clear sense of why she was doing any of it. Her business had grown, but it no longer reflected what truly mattered to her. Her daily grind was not aligned with her deeper values. She even felt distant with the people she loved because, without a strong purpose, she had nothing grounding her.

These fundamental questions within the Purpose Strand will help you illuminate your why:

1. **Mission Clarity**: Do you have a clearly written personal mission statement that guides your daily decisions? Not a corporate document gathering dust, but a living statement that reflects your core values and intentions. Many obstacles arise when our actions do not align with our deeper mission. Like Elena discovered, what looks like an external problem often stems from internal misalignment.

2. **Purpose Definition**: Can you articulate your core purpose in a single, powerful sentence? This isn't about *what* you do; it's about *why* you're here and the impact you want to create. Your purpose should be both inspiring and specific enough to guide real decisions. When Elena finally defined her purpose as "empowering individuals to achieve their highest potential through innovative leadership," it transformed how she approached her team's development.

3. **Values Integration**: Have you identified and written down your nonnegotiable values with clarifying statements? Don't see them as mere words. See them as deeply held principles that filter your decisions. Many obstacles stem from unconsciously compromis-

ing these values. Each value should have clear statements that define how it shows up in your daily life and business.

4. **Achievement Focus**: What is the one goal that would create the most positive impact in your life right now? Not a laundry list of aspirations, but that single breakthrough that would create a ripple effect across everything else. Many people spread their energy across too many goals, diluting their impact and prolonging their obstacles.

5. **Daily Priorities**: Do your first three hours upon waking each day align with your stated purpose, values, and achievement focus? Don't worry about following a "perfect" routine. Instead, see it as protecting your most important activities. Many obstacles persist simply because we react to urgency rather than honoring what is truly important. When Elena started dedicating her peak morning hours to purpose-aligned activities, everything else began falling into place.

When exploring the Purpose Strand, look for:
■ Disconnects between your stated mission and daily actions
■ Values you claim versus values your schedule reflects
■ Areas where you feel energized versus drained
■ Decisions that should be easy given your purpose but feel hard
■ Roles that align with or detract from your core purpose

Document your findings, paying special attention to:
■ Your current personal mission statement (or lack thereof)
■ The clarifying statements for each of your core values
■ How your purpose manifests in each of your key roles
■ Times when you felt most aligned with your purpose
■ Areas where you find yourself making excuses or justifications

When Elena got serious about redefining her purpose, everything started to shift. She restructured her business to reflect her core mission, making decisions that fueled her passion instead of just her bank account. Within two years, she had tripled the size of her business. More importantly, she felt a deep sense of fulfillment for the first time in years. She also reconnected with her family, realizing that being present mattered more than being productive. With a renewed sense of purpose guiding her, every part of her life—work, relationships, and personal fulfillment. Finally, things felt right.

Your purpose isn't just another item on your checklist; it's the compass that makes every other item meaningful. Sometimes what appears to be a practical obstacle is actually a purpose problem in disguise. When your mission is clear, your values are defined, and your purpose is lived daily, many obstacles naturally dissolve or turn into pathways toward creating your dream life.

THE RELATIONSHIPS STRAND: YOUR CONNECTION WEB

Your relationships aren't just about who you know or how many connections you have. They are the invisible threads that weave meaning, support, and growth into every area of your life. Often, what we dismiss as "personality differences" or "bad timing" are actually patterns revealing deeper truths about how we show up in relationships.

Noah was, by all outward measures, crushing it. As a rising executive at a Fortune 500 company, he had mastered the art of professional relationships—or so he thought. His team delivered results, his network was extensive, and his LinkedIn profile was constantly getting offers from recruiters. But at home, a different story was unfolding. His marriage was becoming increasingly distant, his teenage kids were pulling away, and his closest friendships were moving toward surface-level check-ins.

At first, Noah blamed his busy schedule, pointing to the demands of his career and the natural drift that comes with success. But when he examined his Relationships Strand, he discovered an uncomfortable truth: He had been treating all his relationships like business transactions—measuring their value by outcomes rather than genuine connection. His habit of *managing* rather than *engaging* had left him surrounded by people while feeling deeply alone.

The five categories within the Relationship Strand lead to these critical questions:

1. **Clear Communication**: Are you truly expressing yourself? The art of communication doesn't end with being articulate in meetings. It also requires sharing your needs, expectations, and feelings in a clear way. Many relationship obstacles stem from unspoken expectations and assumptions that others "should just know."

2. **Feedback Openness**: Do you invite and accept honest input? This goes beyond annual performance reviews to actively seeking and genuinely considering others' perspectives on how you show up in relationships. When someone gives you feedback, do you take it as a personal attack? Or do you see it as valuable information for growth? Do you express gratitude to that person for bringing this to your attention?

3. **Healthy Boundaries**: Are you protecting your energy? This isn't about building walls but about creating clear limits that allow relationships to thrive. Many people say yes when they want to say no, leading to resentment that poisons otherwise good relationships.

4. **Deep Connections**: Do you have real, honest relationships? This means having at least three people you can talk to about anything—without fear of judgment. Independence is admirable, but isolation disguised as self-sufficiency can leave you emotionally starved.

5. **Conflict Resolution**: Do you face or avoid tough conversations? Without being confrontational, do you address issues directly before they fester? When conflicts arise, do you try to solve them or just hope they go away?

When exploring the Relationships Strand, look for:

- Patterns in how you respond to emotional situations
- Relationships that consistently drain your energy
- Conversations you've been avoiding
- Areas where you feel misunderstood or unheard
- Similarities between personal and professional relationship challenges

Document your findings, paying special attention to:

- Relationships where you feel most/least authentic
- Common feedback you receive across different relationships
- Situations that trigger defensive responses
- Unspoken expectations you hold for others
- Times when you choose silence over honest communication

When Noah finally addressed his relationship patterns, everything shifted. He started with one simple commitment: a sit down dinner (yes, at the dinner table) for an undistracted connection with his family each evening—no phone, no work talk, just presence. He learned to express his needs clearly instead of expecting others to guess them. More importantly, started asking about and listening to his family's needs instead of trying to fix everything. He began treating feedback as a gift rather than a threat to his competence.

Within months, his relationships deepened in ways he hadn't thought possible. His marriage rekindled, his kids started opening up again, and his friendships became genuine sources of joy rather than networking opportunities to maintain. Most surprisingly, his professional relationships improved too—not because he managed them better, but because he finally brought his whole, authentic self to every interaction.

THE GROWTH STRAND:
YOUR EVOLUTION ENGINE

Growth is the fundamental way you approach challenges, setbacks, and opportunities. To limit growth to learning new skills or hitting milestones is missing the mark completely. Stanford psychologist Carol Dweck's research reveals two distinct mindsets: a fixed mindset that believes abilities are static, and a growth mindset that sees capabilities as developable through effort and learning. Often, what we dismiss as "bad luck" or "not being ready" is actually a fixed mindset keeping us trapped in familiar patterns.[1]

Kai had achieved what many would consider the athletic dream. As a former NFL linebacker, he had all the signs of outward success: a Super Bowl ring, Pro Bowl appearances, and a highlight reel that still circulated on social media. But three years into retirement, he felt lost inside. Despite his successful fitness business and regular appearances as a sports commentator, something was missing. His marriage was strained by his restlessness, and his kids seemed more impressed by their friends' startup-founder parents than their dad's old football stories. Each new endeavor felt hollow—like he was just trading on his past rather than truly growing.

At first, he blamed the transition from pro sports, then the demands of business ownership, then the expectations of others. But when he examined his Growth Strand, he discovered something unexpected: His identity as "the former Pro Bowler" had become a prison. He was so focused on maintaining the image of the confident, unbeatable athlete that he had stopped allowing himself to be a beginner at anything new. His past excellence had become a barrier to future growth.

The five categories withing the Growth Strand lead to these critical questions:

1. **Learning Commitment:** Do you dedicate at least fifteen minutes daily to deliberate learning? This isn't about passive content

consumption on TikTok or YouTube, or staying up to date with the news. It's about intentional study and practice in areas that challenge you. Actively reading books while taking notes is the best way to do this. Many obstacles persist simply because we've stopped truly learning.

2. **Challenge Response**: How do you react when facing something you've never done before? It's okay to feel afraid, but it's not okay to stay afraid. Instead, work on your instinctive fear response in situations where you might fail by reframing the situation. Do you automatically look for ways to minimize risk, or do you see the growth opportunity?

3. **Failure Perspective**: Do you reflect on or deflect from your failures? This goes beyond positive thinking to actually extracting lessons from setbacks. Many people do postmortems on their successes but avoid examining their failures, missing crucial growth opportunities.

4. **Skill Development**: Are you actively developing a new skill that makes you uncomfortable? Not just improving what you're already good at, but purposefully tackling areas where you're a beginner. Remember, comfort zones often become cages.

5. **Growth Environment**: Have you surrounded yourself with people who challenge your thinking? This isn't about positive or negative people; it's about having relationships that stretch your perspectives and capabilities. Echo chambers can feel supportive yet they limit your growth.

When exploring the Growth Strand, look for:
- Areas where you consistently avoid challenges
- Skills you have convinced yourself you "can't learn"
- Setbacks that still sting to think about
- Relationships that reinforce your limitations
- Stories you tell yourself about your capabilities

Document your findings, paying special attention to:

- Times when you chose safety over growth
- Patterns in how you respond to criticism
- Skills you have always wanted to learn but haven't started
- People who make you feel simultaneously inspired and uncomfortable
- Areas where past success might be limiting future growth

When Kai finally embraced a growth mindset, everything shifted. He started with one simple commitment: trying one new activity each week where he had no natural advantage. He began taking dance classes, learning to paint, and even studying child psychology after volunteering at an inner-city youth program. He joined groups where no one knew or cared about his NFL career and found himself deeply moved by the challenges facing young athletes from disadvantaged backgrounds.

His whole approach to life transformed. Instead of trying to maintain his image as the unbeatable athlete, he embraced being a beginner again. His business evolved from just sports training to a comprehensive youth development program, combining athletics with emotional intelligence and academic support. His commentary became more insightful, his family life was more connected, and he found a new kind of confidence—not from being the best, but from the impact he could have on the next generation while continuing to grow himself.

THE RESOURCES STRAND: YOUR SUPPORT SYSTEM

Your resources are about how effectively you deploy what is available to you. Often, what we dismiss as "lack of time" or "insufficient support" is actually an underutilization of the tools and systems already within our reach.

Zara seemed to have everything needed for success. As a talented consultant with an impressive client list, extensive industry knowledge, and numerous opportunities, she should have been thriving. Instead, she felt constantly overwhelmed, missing deadlines and opportunities while watching others with seemingly fewer advantages surge ahead. Her carefully crafted to-do lists and productivity apps weren't translating into actual results.

At first, she blamed her workload, then her clients' demands, then her lack of support staff. But when she examined her Resources Strand, she discovered something unexpected: She had been collecting tools without building systems. Her workplace was filled with productivity apps, planners, and equipment, but she lacked the frameworks to make them work together effectively. She was trying to build success on a foundation of scattered resources rather than integrated systems.

The five categories in the Resources Strand lead to these critical questions:

1. **Strategic Planning**: Do you have a proven system for weekly planning and daily execution? Forget about only relying on to-do lists. It's time you create a reliable framework for turning intentions into results, including matching your most important work to your peak energy hours. Many obstacles persist because we confuse planning with productivity.

2. **Feedback & Measurement**: How do you track success in each key area of life? Don't obsess over numbers. Have clear indicators of progress. Without measurement, you will rely on gut feelings rather than real data. The most successful people track specific metrics across health (sleep, workouts, medical check-ups), wealth (income, investments, spending), relationships (quality time, meaningful interactions), and career (income, productivity, learning progress).

3. **Decision Optimization**: Do you use specific frameworks to analyze decisions? You need reliable tools that cut through confusion. The Eisenhower Matrix helps you decide what to do next by sorting tasks based on urgency and importance, perfect for daily prioritization. The 10-10-10 Rule helps with bigger decisions by analyzing how you'll feel about the choice in 10 minutes, 10 months, and 10 years, ideal for clarity on long-term impact.[2] Many obstacles stem from emotional or rushed decisions that could have been avoided with these simple frameworks.

4. **Accountability Systems**: Who or what keeps you consistently on track? Willpower won't see you through. Instead, create external structures that ensure follow-through. Even the most disciplined people need systematic accountability through coaches, mastermind groups, or tracking systems.

5. **Environmental Design**: Does your physical and digital environment support or sabotage your success? Having a perfect workspace does not guarantee success. But you can intentionally design your surroundings so that it's easier to make good choices and distractions harder to access.

When exploring the Resources Strand, look for:

■ Systems you have been avoiding but know would help
■ Areas where you are guessing instead of measuring
■ Decisions you have made impulsively rather than strategically
■ People who influence your behavior—positively or negatively
■ Environmental cues that push you toward or away from success

Document your findings, paying special attention to:

■ Your current planning routine (or lack thereof)
■ Metrics you are tracking versus ones you should be tracking
■ How you currently make major decisions
■ Who holds you accountable (if anyone)
■ Ways your environment either supports or sabotages your goals

When Zara finally optimized her Resources Strand, everything shifted. She started with one simple commitment: implementing a "Sunday System" where she planned each week using the Eisenhower Matrix, matching her most important work to her peak morning hours. She then started using the 10-10-10 Rule on the most important things she had to work on to decide if they belonged on her calendar at all.

She created simple tracking dashboards for her key life areas and moved her phone to another room during deep work blocks. She found a coach, then joined a weekly mastermind group that kept her accountable to her highest priorities. Within months, her productivity doubled—not because she worked more hours, but because she finally had systems that made success inevitable. Her client results improved, her stress decreased, and she found herself achieving in one quarter what used to take a year, all by optimizing the resources and systems already available to her.

FINDING YOUR HIDDEN TRUTH

You have now explored the five strands of O-DNA, and you've seen how one core issue can manifest across multiple areas. Simon discovered his leadership challenges weren't about strategy but sleep. Elena's turnover problem revealed a deeper purpose misalignment. Kai's identity crisis opened the door to genuine growth. Noah's relationship patterns pointed to his need to control rather than connect. Zara's productivity struggles weren't about effort but systems.

Each story reveals a powerful truth: You are not looking for five different problems to solve. You are searching for the ONE thing—the hidden truth that explains why your current obstacle persists despite your best efforts. If the solution was obvious, you would have found it already. That's why O-DNA requires honest exploration. As you review your findings, pay special attention to what made you defensive, what you dismissed as "just the way it is," and what connections you hadn't considered before.

Sometimes, the most powerful breakthrough comes not from finding the answer, but from finally being ready to hear it. Don't ask, "What's wrong in each area of my life?" Ask, "What ONE thing, once addressed, will create positive change across ALL areas?"

KEY TAKEAWAYS

- **The Hidden Truth Principle**
  - Surface obstacles often mask deeper patterns.
  - What looks like a business problem might be a health issue.
  - What feels like a resource gap might be a purpose misalignment.
  - What appears as relationship tension might stem from growth resistance.
- **The Power of Systematic Discovery**
  - Each O-DNA strand reveals a different perspective on the same truth.
  - Success leaves clues across all five areas of life.
  - Your strongest resistance often points to your greatest opportunity.
  - Small changes in root causes create large effects across all areas.
- **The ONE Thing Focus**
  - The goal isn't to fix everything. The goal is to find the ONE key that unlocks everything.
  - Transformation comes from addressing causes, not symptoms.
  - Real breakthroughs often appear in unexpected places.
  - Your blind spots exist for a reason; they protect deeper truths.

REFLECTION QUESTIONS

1. Discovery Depth

- Which story (Simon, Elena, Kai, Mark, or Zara) resonated most with you and why?

....

....

- What patterns emerged as you explored your health, purpose, relationships, growth, and resources?

....

....

- Where do you find yourself making the same excuses across different areas?

....

....

- What "reasonable explanations" might be masking deeper truths?

....

....

2. Pattern Recognition

- How do your health patterns affect your leadership?

....

....

- Where does your purpose (or lack thereof) show up in your relationships?

....

....

■ How does your growth mindset impact your resource utilization?

■ What connections between strands surprised you most?

3. Breakthrough Preparation

■ What one change could positively impact all five O-DNA strands?

■ Which area feels simultaneously most challenging and most promising?

■ What truth have you been avoiding that might be ready to face?

■ Who could help you validate your discoveries?

ACTION STEPS

1. **Complete Your O-DNA Strand Analysis**
   - Take the health baseline assessment.
   - Write your purpose statement and clarifying values.
   - Map your key relationships and communication patterns.
   - Document your growth versus fixed mindset responses.
   - Audit your current systems and resource utilization.

   ....

   ....

   ....

   ....

2. **Connect Your Discoveries**
   - Create a mind map linking challenges across strands.
   - Identify recurring themes in your responses.
   - List situations where multiple strands intersect.
   - Note areas where improvement in one strand might uplift others.

   ....

   ....

   ....

   ....

   ....

   ....

3. Prepare for Deep Work

- Start your breakthrough journal.
- Select your ONE thing to focus on.
- Gather evidence of patterns you have noticed.
- List specific questions for your support network.

4. Set up Success Systems

- Choose your decision-making framework (Eisenhower or 10-10-10).
- Establish your measurement metrics.
- Create your accountability structure.
- Design your optimal environment.

LOOKING AHEAD

Finding your root cause through O-DNA is powerful, but it is only the first step. Our blind spots exist for a reason—they often protect us from uncomfortable truths or challenging changes. That's why the next chapter is crucial. We will explore how to take your discovery outside your sphere of influence, connecting with others who can help validate your findings and strengthen your resolve for change.

A GOOD COACH WILL MAKE
HIS PLAYERS SEE WHAT
THEY CAN BE RATHER THAN
WHAT THEY ARE.

**—Ara Parseghian, Hall of Fame
football coach**

CHAPTER 5

Connect: Share Your Discovery

———

WHEN SURGEONS FACE THEIR MOST challenging cases, they don't just consult with colleagues down the hall. They reach out to specialists at other hospitals, present at international conferences, and seek insights from experts across the globe. They know that breakthroughs often come from perspectives outside their immediate circle—from doctors who are not caught in the same thought patterns or bound by the same institutional assumptions. Yet in business and within our personal lives, we often try to solve our biggest challenges on our own or by consulting only those within our sphere of influence—the very people who share our blind spots and biases.

In the RCD Method, the Connect stage is about breaking free from the Blame Loop by seeking wisdom from outside your sphere of influence. This is crucial because the people closest to your situation—your team, family, friends, or advisors—are often caught in the same patterns of Blind Blaming that you are.

Think about it: If everyone in your current sphere could see the root cause of your obstacle, wouldn't they have pointed it out already? Most of the time they've already tried and given you their advice. The truth is, they are often too close, too invested, or too entangled in the same patterns to offer truly transformative insight. This is why the Connect stage in the RCD Method relies on two distinct forces that must come from outside your regular sphere of influence:

THE RCD METHOD ™

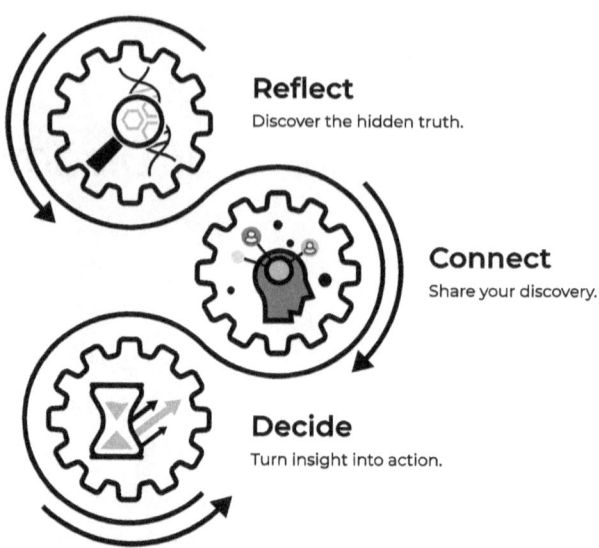

Reflect
Discover the hidden truth.

Connect
Share your discovery.

Decide
Turn insight into action.

1. **The Catalyst**: *Your Professional Coach.* A catalyst is an agent that provokes significant change or action. Like a chemical catalyst that accelerates reactions without being consumed, your coach creates the conditions for breakthroughs without solving your problems for you. Because they are outside your sphere of influence, they can:

   - See patterns that everyone inside your sphere has normalized.
   - Ask questions that those close to you won't ask.
   - Challenge assumptions that your regular circle shares.
   - Push past the comfortable explanations everyone has accepted.
   - Hold yourself accountable without being entangled in your current dynamics.

2. **The Collective**: *Your Mastermind Group.* A collective combines the power of multiple perspectives, experiences, and insights from people who are not caught in your current situation. Your master-

mind group acts as a living laboratory where ideas are tested, assumptions are challenged, and breakthroughs are forged through the wisdom of shared experience. Because they are outside your sphere of influence, they can:

■ Spot patterns that your current circle has become blind to.

■ Share solutions that worked in similar but different contexts.

■ Challenge your thinking without personal agenda.

■ Offer feedback untainted by office politics or family dynamics.

■ Provide accountability without being invested in your status quo.

Together, these external forces create a powerful environment for transformation. The Catalyst accelerates your journey by helping you see what everyone in your sphere has been missing, while the Collective provides the real-world wisdom to validate and enhance your insights from a position of objective experience. One sparks the breakthrough; the other helps to ensure it sticks. The key is that both forces must come from outside the sphere where your obstacle exists.

Reflect, Then Connect

Kristen sat across from her coach, spreading out her O-DNA worksheet. Her business had been hovering just below $750,000 in revenue for three years straight. After weeks of reflection, she thought she had found her root cause: She needed to hire a new salesperson who was underperforming so the company could break through to seven figures. The solution seemed obvious: A new sales staff that "can sell" equals more revenue. But she kept hesitating, worried about the investment. "I know I need someone good, but I can't afford to pay market rate until they prove themselves," she explained. "What if it doesn't work out?"

That's when her coach asked one simple question: "I notice you keep saying you need someone else to get you to a million, but you are not willing to invest in that person until they are already successful. What if it's not actually about the money?" The question hung in the air. Before Kristen could answer, her coach continued. "Looking at your O-DNA, I see a pattern. You're not really looking for a salesperson. You're looking for permission to grow bigger. Every strand shows you putting a ceiling on what is possible. You're afraid to invest in a great salesperson because, deep down, you are not convinced you deserve to be at that level."

Later that week in her mastermind group, another business owner leaned forward to speak. "You know what this reminds me of? Where I was two years ago. I kept saying I needed more salespeople to grow, but I wasn't willing to pay enough to attract real talent. I told myself it was about being financially responsible. Truthfully, I was hiding behind hiring. I had secretly convinced myself that seven figures was for other people, not for me. Every time I got close, I'd find a reason why I needed someone else to get me there. But I had made sure they couldn't succeed by underpaying them."

This is the power of strategic connection. What looks like a hiring or performance issue through our own lens often takes on new meaning when viewed through the eyes of others outside our sphere of influence. Kristen's O-DNA results had revealed patterns, but it took perspectives from beyond her usual circle—people not caught in her same thought patterns—to see that her "need to hire" was actually masking a deeper truth: She had unconsciously decided that certain levels of success were not available to her.

The real root cause wasn't about needing another salesperson; it was about the limiting beliefs she held about her own potential. She had been using hiring as a way to avoid facing these beliefs, creating a perfect excuse for why she couldn't grow further on her own. By undervaluing the role and refusing to invest in this person properly, she was setting up each hiring attempt to fail, reinforcing her hidden belief that bigger success wasn't meant for her.

The Catalyst: Why You Need a Coach

Have you ever seen someone reach world-class performance—in any field—without a coach? Olympic athletes, Fortune 500 CEOs, and Grammy-winning musicians all have coaches. Not because they are not talented or capable, but because they understand a fundamental truth: You cannot see your own blind spots. Coaches help you do things you normally wouldn't do to get better.

Think of your coach as your catalyst for breakthrough.

- Coaches get in the trenches with you.
- Coaches dig deep to uncover what is really holding you back.
- Coaches push you past your comfortable excuses.
- Coaches help you see negative patterns you have normalized.
- Coaches hold you accountable to your highest potential.

Let me share a story about consultants and catalysts (coaches) that I heard from my friend Brendan. A man was driving through the countryside when he noticed a large flock of sheep grazing in a field. Intrigued, he stopped his car and approached the shepherd, who was tending to the flock. The man, eager to demonstrate his expertise, said, "If I can tell you exactly how many sheep are in your flock, will you give me one of them?"

The shepherd, skeptical but curious, agreed. "Sure, why not?"

The man pulled out his laptop, connected to his phone, and ran complex algorithms with the help of GPS and AI-based software. After a few minutes, he announced, "You have exactly one thousand two hundred forty-seven sheep."

The shepherd, impressed, said, "That is correct. Go ahead and take one."

The consultant selected one, put it in the trunk of his car, and prepared to leave. But before he could drive off, the shepherd stopped him. "Wait a moment! If I can guess your profession, will you give it back?"

The consultant, amused, replied, "Sure, go ahead."

The shepherd confidently said, "You're a consultant."

108 | BEYOND BLIND BLAMING

The consultant, taken aback, asked, "How did you know?"

The shepherd smiled and replied, "Three reasons: First, you came uninvited. Second, you told me something I already knew. And third, you don't understand anything about me or my business. Now will you please put my *dog* back and leave?"

The point? A consultant gives you answers. A catalyst, or coach, helps you discover your own truth. They also see who you can be, not who you are currently.

The Collective: Your Mastermind Group

In his landmark 1937 book *Think and Grow Rich*, Napoleon Hill introduced a concept that would revolutionize how successful people approach growth. After studying hundreds of the world's most successful individuals—including Andrew Carnegie, Henry Ford, and Thomas Edison—Hill discovered a common thread: None of them achieved success alone. They all participated in what he called a "Master Mind" alliance.

Hill defined the mastermind principle as: "The coordination of knowledge and effort of two or more people who work toward a definite purpose, in the spirit of harmony." He observed that when a group of minds come together in harmony, they create a "third mind"—a master mind—that each participant can draw upon.[1]

This isn't just philosophical theory. Hill also noted that every major fortune began with the formation of a mastermind alliance. Carnegie attributed his entire fortune to the power of his mastermind group, which he called his "brain trust." Edison regularly collaborated with other brilliant minds in his Menlo Park laboratory, creating an environment where breakthrough ideas could flourish.

Today, your mastermind group serves as your breakthrough collective—a community of peers outside your sphere of influence who can look at your O-DNA insights with fresh eyes and relevant experience. Unlike professional coaches who catalyze transformation from a trained perspective, your collective brings the power of lived experience and shared wisdom.

Think of it as having a personal board of advisors who:

- Challenge your assumptions from experience
- Share battle-tested solutions
- Offer real-world pattern recognition
- Provide genuine accountability
- Create a community of growth

This phenomenon explains why Kristen's breakthrough came not just from hearing others' experiences, but from the collective wisdom that emerged when multiple perspectives focused on her challenge. Her mastermind group didn't only offer advice. They created an environment where new possibilities could emerge.

Your mastermind group should:

1. Meet regularly with structured agendas.
2. Include members at or above your level.
3. Represent diverse experiences but similar ambitions.
4. Maintain strict confidentiality.
5. Hold each other accountable for growth.

Hill emphasized that the selection of your mastermind group is crucial. He advised choosing members who bring:

- Knowledge you don't possess
- Experience in areas where you seek growth
- A spirit of generosity in sharing insights
- Unwavering commitment to mutual success
- The courage to speak hard truths

Most importantly, your mastermind must come from outside your sphere of influence. Remember, the people caught in the same patterns as you—your team, regular advisors, or industry peers—often share your blind spots. True breakthrough requires fresh perspectives from minds that are not entangled in your current situation.

This is why successful people often belong to multiple mastermind groups, each serving a different purpose:

- Industry-specific groups for tactical insights
- Cross-industry groups for broader perspective
- High-level groups for strategic thinking
- Personal development groups for holistic growth

The power of a mastermind group isn't only in the advice you receive; it's in the exponential growth that happens when minds unite in pursuit of breakthrough.

Finding Your Forces of Connection

"I know I need help, but I have no idea where to start." I hear this constantly from business owners, professionals, and friends all the time. They have reached a plateau and face an unresolved obstacle, or there is a goal they have been unable to reach. They know something needs to change, but the world of professional coaching and mastermind groups feels foreign and overwhelming. Let me demystify both and show you exactly how to find the right support for your breakthrough.

Understanding Business and Life Coaching

A professional coach serves as a catalyst for your personal insights and growth, rather than acting as a consultant who provides direct instructions, or a mentor who shares personal experiences. The essence of coaching lies in its transformative approach: Through powerful questioning, coaches help illuminate your blind spots and guide you toward discovering solutions that already exist within you. They maintain unwavering accountability while leading you through proven growth frameworks, all while challenging the limiting assumptions and beliefs that may be holding you back.

Experience and a proven track record fundamentally distinguish exceptional coaches from those who merely claim the title. A truly qualified coach brings several crucial elements to the relationship: a proven methodology for creating breakthroughs, well-documented success stories from previous clients, specialized expertise in your specific challenges, professional training with appropriate certifications, and a clear process for measuring and tracking results.

The process of selecting the right coach transcends considerations of popularity or cost. Instead, focus on finding someone with expertise in your specific field, experience working with individuals at your level and beyond, a proven track record of facilitating similar achievements, deep understanding of your industry's unique challenges, and the ability to provide references from clients who have overcome comparable obstacles.

Consider Kristen's breakthrough as an example. Her success stemmed from working with a coach who understood business growth broadly and specifically comprehended the unique challenges of scaling service businesses beyond the $750,000 threshold. This specialized expertise enabled them to identify patterns that might have eluded a general business coach.

Understanding Mastermind Groups

While coaching provides individualized guidance, mastermind groups offer the power of collective wisdom. However, not every group that identifies with the mastermind title truly qualifies for this designation. Authentic mastermind groups operate with regular, structured meetings and have a carefully curated membership of peers at similar levels. They also maintain strict confidentiality protocols, proven problem-solving frameworks, and systems for creating measurable results for all participants. The key distinction between a networking group and a genuine mastermind lies in its leadership and structure. A properly orchestrated mastermind incorporates professional facilitation, established protocols for exchanging feedback, robust accountability mechanisms, comprehensive progress tracking systems, and regular evaluation of the group's effectiveness.

The ideal collective brings together peers operating at or above your level, members from diverse backgrounds but aligned growth trajectories, industry-specific focus or shared challenges, strong facilitation to maintain momentum and value, and regular, structured meetings with clear objectives. Remember that the value derived from your mastermind typically correlates directly with your investment level—free or low-cost groups often lack the commitment and structure necessary for achieving significant breakthroughs.

The Challenge of Finding a Quality Mastermind Group

Here is an uncomfortable truth: The majority of coaches and mastermind groups lack the necessary experience and structure to facilitate genuine breakthroughs. Too many people invest their time and resources in coaches who haven't achieved what they are teaching. They join masterminds that function merely as social gatherings. I see too many people wasting money on programs without defined methodologies, groups lacking proper facilitation, and connections that fail to drive meaningful results.

This prevalent quality gap inspired the creation of our specialized matching system at www.BlindBlaming.com/connect. We have undertaken the rigorous work of vetting coaches for proven experience, establishing structured mastermind protocols, facilitating appropriate matches between individuals and their support systems, ensuring consistent quality and accountability, and implementing comprehensive results tracking.

The Investment Question

"How much does it cost?" This is often the first question people ask about coaching and mastermind groups. And I get it. When you hear that top business coaches charge anywhere from $50,000 to $250,000 per year, and premium mastermind groups can range from $50,000 to $500,000 annually, it's natural to experience sticker shock.

But let's reframe this question: What is the cost of staying stuck? Kristen initially balked at paying market rate ($80,000 base plus commission) for a top-tier sales professional. Yet she was losing far more by staying stuck at $750,000 in revenue. What's even more telling? She willingly invested $5,000 monthly in high-level coaching and $50,000 annually in a premium mastermind group. Why? Because she understood something crucial about breakthrough: The right external perspective is priceless.

I want to make something very clear: We all have different budgets and income levels. I strongly believe you should never go into debt to hire a coach or join a mastermind group. If you can't pay in full or cover it with 3 monthly payments without financial strain, wait until you can. Growth requires pushing your comfort zone, but not at the expense of financial stability. There are coaching and mastermind options at various price points - you can start with more affordable programs and graduate to higher-level investments as your income and success grow. The right program for you exists at your current financial level.

Here is what successful people understand about investing in connection:

1. Return on Investment

- A single insight from the right coach can create millions in new revenue or income.
- One connection from a quality mastermind group can open untapped markets.
- Breaking through one limiting belief can exponentially expand your business or your life.
- The right guidance can save years of costly trial and error.

2. The Real Cost Comparison

- What is another year at your current revenue or income worth?
- How much are your current limitations costing in missed opportunities?

- What is the price of making the same mistakes others have already solved?
- How valuable is time lost trying to figure everything out alone?

3. Investment vs. Expense

- Coaching and masterminds are not line-item expenses.
- They are investments in expanding your possibilities.
- The return often comes in multiples, not percentages.
- The transformation affects all areas of life and business.

Think about world-class athletes. They don't question investing in elite coaches—they know their success depends on it. Top performers in any field understand that breakthrough requires investment in high-level support.

Consider these real examples:

- A business owner hesitated to invest $60,000 in a premium mastermind. After joining, one connection led to a $2.5 million contract.

- An entrepreneur questioned spending $8,000 monthly on a top coach. Within six months, their revenue tripled.

- A professional resisted the $40,000 investment in a high-level group. One strategic partnership formed there resulted in a $5 million acquisition.

Here's the reality: Quality coaching and masterminds aren't cheap because they are not designed to be. They are priced to:

- Ensure full commitment from participants
- Attract high-level peers and expertise
- Create environments for real breakthrough
- Deliver transformative results
- Provide maximum value and support

One of my favorite quotes is simply, "People who pay, pay attention."

That's why I advise people to avoid *free* coaches and masterminds because the value usually isn't there.

The question isn't, "Can I afford this?" The real questions are:

- "Can I afford to stay stuck?"
- "What is breakthrough actually worth to me?"
- "How much longer will I try to do this alone?"
- "What is the cost of delayed transformation?"

Price is what you pay. Value is what you get. And transformation? That is priceless.

Making Connection Work

The most powerful connections in the world won't help if you're not ready to show up and do the work. The most successful coaching clients and mastermind group members have these things in common:

- They are ready for real transformation.
- They are committed to their breakthrough.
- They are willing to be challenged.
- They are prepared to invest in themselves.
- They are determined to create results.

If that sounds like you, keep reading! Let's explore how to make the Connect phase of the RCD Method truly transformative once you've found the right coach and mastermind group.

WORKING WITH COACHES: THE BREAKTHROUGH FRAMEWORK

The following seven elements of the Breakthrough Framework are the foundation of transformative coaching relationships. When you treat coaching sessions as optional or squeeze them into busy days without preparation, you are signaling to yourself and your coach that breakthrough is a "nice to have" luxury rather than a necessity.

I have seen countless clients struggle to gain traction simply because they approached coaching casually, treating it like just another meeting. When things don't work out, they usually blame the coach for their lack of results, but typically, the client is at the center of the issue. Once again, they are stuck in the Blame Loop.

The most successful clients I've worked with do the opposite. They guard their coaching time fiercely, arrive thoroughly prepared, and take full ownership of their growth journey. They understand that the magic doesn't happen in the coaching session itself; it happens in the preparation, reflection, and implementation between sessions.

One of my recent memories with a coaching client is when Sally said, "I need to cancel our call. I have a $6,000 sale coming in." She was too focused on short-term fixes rather than long-term results. The agenda items I had prepared for her that day were going to make her another $250,000. What do you think is more important? (This is *not* a trick question.) Your coach might be world-class, but if you are checking emails during sessions or constantly rescheduling or canceling, you are sabotaging your own breakthrough.

Remember: Your coach is investing their expertise and energy in your success. The least you can do is match that investment with your commitment and preparation.

Before Every Session:

1. **Prepare**: Do you schedule coaching sessions before anything else on your calendar? Not fitting them in when convenient but protecting them as sacred time.

2. **Do the Deep Work**: Do you spend at least thirty minutes preparing for each session? Not just showing up but arriving with clear focus and specific questions.

3. **Review Your O-DNA**: Do you regularly update your analysis based on new insights? Not sticking to first impressions, but letting your understanding evolve.

4. **Document Progress**: Do you track changes and patterns between sessions? Not just noting actions but observing how changes affect multiple areas.

5. **Create Space**: Are you distraction-free during sessions? Not multitasking but giving your breakthrough full attention.

6. **Follow Through**: Do you implement the insights and actions discussed? Not just having good conversations but taking decisive action on what you learn.

7. **Take Responsibility**: Do you own your growth journey completely? Not relying on your coach to drive progress, but taking full ownership of your transformation.

Maximizing Masterminds: The Connection Framework

The Connection Framework for masterminds is equally crucial but often overlooked. Many people join mastermind groups with the same casual attitude they bring to networking events, then wonder why they are not seeing results. A powerful mastermind isn't just a gathering of peers. It's a carefully orchestrated environment for transformation. Each element of this framework builds on the others. Without proper group selection, even perfect attendance won't yield results. Without vulnerability, thorough preparation becomes merely an academic exercise. Without implementation focus, the most insightful discussions remain theoretical.

And without taking responsibility for your impact on the group, you diminish the very power of collective wisdom that you joined to access. The most successful mastermind participants I have seen treat these elements as nonnegotiable commitments. They understand that the group's transformation potential multiplies when every member brings their full selves to the process.

Think of it this way: In a group of eight people, when you show up unprepared or skip a session, you are not just cheating yourself. You are depriving seven other people of your unique perspective and contribution to their breakthrough.

Here are some tips to get the most out of your mastermind experience and get the results you desire.

1. **Group Selection**: Are you part of a mastermind that challenges your thinking? Not just networking, but deep, transformative connection.

2. **Regular Engagement**: Do you attend and participate fully in every session? Not just showing up but being fully present and engaged.

3. **Preparation Depth**: Do you prepare thoroughly for each mastermind meeting? Not winging it but bringing real value to every session.

4. **Vulnerability Level**: Do you share your true challenges, not just your successes? Not performing but being authentically open.

5. **Implementation Focus**: Do you act on the insights you receive? Not just collecting ideas but testing and applying them.

6. **Contribute Generously**: Do you actively support the growth of other members? Contributing to the community rather than only benefiting from it.

7. **Take Responsibility**: Do you honor your commitment to the group? Not letting the collective down but strengthening it through reliable participation.

The synergy between these frameworks—coaching and masterminds—creates an unstoppable force for transformation. Your coach helps you see what you have been missing, while your mastermind group provides the real-world testing ground for your insights. Together, they form a complete support system for breakthrough, but only if you show up fully committed to both relationships. Half-hearted participation in either one undermines the potential of both. When you fully engage with these frameworks, you create an environment where breakthrough becomes not just possible, but inevitable.

KEY TAKEAWAYS

- Breaking free from the Blame Loop requires perspectives from outside your sphere of influence—from people who are not caught in the same patterns and blind spots as you.

- The Connect stage relies on two crucial external forces: The Catalyst (your professional coach) and the Collective (your mastermind group). Each serves a distinct purpose in creating breakthrough.

- A professional coach acts as a catalyst by seeing patterns others miss, asking uncomfortable questions, and holding you accountable without being entangled in your current dynamics.

- Your mastermind group provides collective wisdom through shared experiences, offering solutions from different contexts and feedback untainted by office politics or personal agendas.

- The investment in coaching and mastermind groups should be viewed through the lens of transformation value rather than just monetary cost because the price of staying stuck often far exceeds the investment in growth.

- Quality connections require both finding the right support and showing up prepared to do the work. The most powerful coach or mastermind group can't help if you're not ready for transformation.

REFLECTION QUESTIONS _____

1. Who are the people currently in your sphere of influence that you typically turn to for advice? How might they share your blind spots?

....

....

2. Think about your biggest current challenge. What perspectives might you be missing by staying within your usual circle of advisors?

....

....

....

....

3. What beliefs do you hold about investing in your own growth? Are these beliefs serving your highest potential?

....

....

....

....

4. How have you historically approached seeking an outside perspective? What patterns do you notice in when and how you seek help?

....

....

....

....

5. What would becoming "unstuck" be worth to you? What is the real cost of maintaining your current limitations?

....

....

6. How ready are you to be challenged by perspectives that might contradict your current understanding of your situation?

....

....

....

....

ACTION STEPS

1. Complete Your Connection Audit

- List everyone you currently turn to for advice.
- Note their relationship to your situation.
- Identify potential shared blind spots.
- Assess the diversity of perspectives you are receiving.

....

....

....

....

2. Define Your Ideal Support System

- Write down the specific expertise you need.
- Identify gaps in your current advisory network.
- Research potential coaches in your field.
- Explore mastermind groups that are above your level.

....

....

....

3. Calculate Your "Stuck Cost"

- Quantify what your current limitations cost you.
- Project the value of potential breakthrough.
- Research appropriate investment levels for support.
- Create a transformation budget.

....

....

....

....

....

4. Prepare for Connection

- Set aside dedicated time for growth work.
- Create a system for tracking insights and progress.
- Establish clear objectives for external support.
- Commit to specific preparation protocols.

....

....

....

....

....

LOOKING AHEAD

In the next chapter, we will explore the final stage of the RCD Method: Decide. Now that you have done the deep work of Reflection and found powerful Connection support, you are ready to make decisions that stick.

You will discover that true decision-making isn't just about choosing a path. It's about creating the conditions where your new choices become inevitable. With your reflections clear and your connections strong, you are ready to make decisions that transform your life and business.

THE QUALITY OF YOUR LIFE
IS BUILT ON THE QUALITY
OF YOUR DECISIONS.

—Wesam Fawz, international business
growth strategist

CHAPTER 6

Decide: Turn Insight into Action

———

THE RCD METHOD™

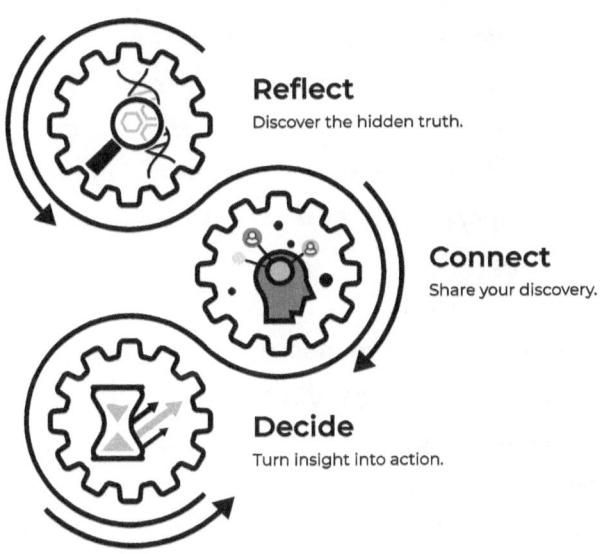

Reflect
Discover the hidden truth.

Connect
Share your discovery.

Decide
Turn insight into action.

THE LAST STAGE OF THE TRANSFORMATIVE RCD Method is Decide, which deals with the power of decision-making. Before I dive in, though, I want to discuss the power of *language*. My friend Erik shared a story that perfectly explains why I decided to steer this chapter in a . . . Well, let's just say a more verbally *fluent* direction. But trust me. It's all for the sake of getting real and initiating lasting results. Erik used to get extremely offended by people using profanity, which caused him to avoid those who cursed and refuse to read books containing "bad" language. Until he made a pivotal realization: "I've been letting someone else's word choices keep me from potentially life-changing wisdom—in books, podcasts, lectures, and even with certain friends. I've been so hung up on letters arranged in a certain order that I have avoided a lot of ways to expand and simply get real. How ridiculous is that?"

Erik refused to filter out what some consider to be offensive in order to hear the foundational truth of someone's message. Why? Because he simply didn't like their delivery. Are F-bombs and such necessary? Possibly! And sometimes no! Depends on the motivation and passion behind *why* someone uses them. To toss them around casually and speak crudely is never a good look. With that I will concede. As a kid, did your mother ever use your *full name* when she was trying to get your attention because you needed to listen for your well-being and safety? Your ears perked up, didn't they? You stood at full attention. Same thought process here. When used for impact, some profanity might highlight that it's time to wake up and listen!

In this chapter, you'll encounter what some might consider strong language—specifically, one very direct phrase I use purposefully and intentionally. It's not for shock value or casual effect. I believe that sometimes, a powerful truth requires powerful language.

Interestingly, research supports this approach. Studies have shown that people who use profanity tend to be more honest and trustworthy and maintain stronger relationships. A 2017 study in the *Social Psychological and Personality Science* journal found that people who curse tend to be more authentic in their expression and have higher levels of integrity. In fact, they are less likely to lie or deceive for social desirability.[1]

But here's the deal: If strong language bothers you, I completely respect that. You have two choices: Either put this book down and find a gentler guide, or, like Erik, decide that you won't let someone's word choices keep you from a potential mindset breakthrough.

The last step in the RCD Method you are about to read is real, raw, and transformative. Therefore the language I use matches the gravity of the insights it contains. Your growth is too substantial to water down the truth.

Let's go!

A STORY ABOUT DECISIVE LEADERSHIP

A general walked into a room where two teams had spent a year researching different solutions to a complex problem. Team A and Team B presented their findings for about forty-five minutes. After listening to both sides, the general quickly chose Solution A. His assistant was baffled.

Months later, he asked the general, "Sir, what ever happened with that meeting where you helped those two teams after a year of research? I was a little surprised at how quickly you made that decision considering they'd been researching the problem for over a year. You chose Solution A if I remember correctly."

The general shrugged and said, "I don't remember. Somebody just needed to make a fucking decision!"

This is what the final step of the RCD Method is all about. You've done the reflection. You've got an outside perspective. Now it's time to Make a Fucking Decision (MFD) and move forward. This is what the final step of the RCD Method™ is all about.

Why Decisions Get Stuck

Here is the pathway that well-intentioned people go down when they experience decision-making paralysis:

- You see the real problem clearly through O-DNA (Reflect).
- You get valuable outside perspective (Connect).
- Then, you hesitate. You analyze. You wait.
- And nothing changes.

The Power of MFD

In order to Make a Fucking Decision, you must do more than choose. You must also break free from the paralysis that keeps you stuck. We live in a world that celebrates endless analysis, perfect information, and universal agreement. But here's the truth: Breakthroughs don't come from perfect analysis. They come from *decisive action*.

Think about the most successful people you know. What sets them apart isn't superior intelligence or better information. It's their ability to make clear decisions and fully commit to them. While others are still analyzing, debating, and seeking consensus, they are taking action and learning from the results—positive or negative.

When you Make a Fucking Decision, you are able to step into your power as a decision-maker. It means no more hiding behind analysis paralysis, waiting for perfect certainty, trying to please everyone, and using "what-ifs" as an excuse for inaction. It means choosing a direction and committing to it with everything you've got.

Consider Kristen's journey again. She had all the data. She had insights from her O-DNA. She had guidance from her coach and mastermind group. But none of that mattered until she made a fucking decision to step into a bigger vision for herself and her business. The moment she decided—truly decided—everything changed.

Three elements are required when you Make a Fucking Decision, each building on the insights you've gained through the Reflect and Connect stage. First, you must identify the real obstacle. Not the surface issue you started with. Not what others think the problem is. Not even what you initially believed was holding you back. You must name the truth you have uncovered through your O-DNA analysis and validate it through an outside perspective. For Kristen, this meant acknowledging that her limiting beliefs, not her hiring needs, were the real obstacle.

Second, you must choose your path forward. This isn't about finding the perfect solution; it's about choosing a clear direction based on what you've learned. Progress over perfection. Your choice should be informed by your reflection and the wisdom you've gained from coaches and masterminds. Ultimately, though, it must be your decision to do something. The path must be clear and actionable, something you can begin immediately.

Finally, and most crucially, you must fucking commit. This is where most people falter. They make decisions with hedges and escape clauses, keeping one foot on the dock while trying to step into the boat. That's not commitment. That is hesitation dressed up as decision-making. Real commitment means no hedging, no half measures, no backup plans that undermine your primary path. It means burning the boats and going all in.

The power of MFD lies not in the decision itself, but in the clarity and energy it creates. When you truly decide—when you Make a Fucking Decision with full commitment—you end the energy drain of uncertainty. You stop the waste of mental resources on "maybes" and "what-ifs." You free yourself to focus entirely on making your decision work. When a decision doesn't work out as planned, simply pivot, adapt, and learn from the experience. Every outcome, whether desired or not, teaches us something valuable. Instead of viewing unexpected results as failures, treat them as data points guiding you toward a better approach. It is far better to make a choice and learn from the experience than to remain paralyzed by indecision, forever wondering, *What if this or that happens?*

This is why successful people emphasize that making a decision and moving forward is far more important than the specific choice itself. They understand that if things don't go as planned, they can adjust, overcome, and ultimately conquer any challenges they face. As Julius Caesar famously declared: "*Veni, vidi, vici.*" I came, I saw, I conquered.

At a recent mastermind meeting we sponsored, the group came up with something I loved after my presentation and group exercise: MFD and DES. Make a Fucking Decision, and you'll Do Epic Shit. Remember that. There might have been wine and liquor involved, but the group loved it. A good decision executed with complete conviction will almost always outperform a perfect decision executed with hesitation—or worse, never executed at all.

WHAT DECISION-MAKING LOOKS LIKE IN ACTION

Let's see how Kristen finally broke through:

Starting Problem: "I need to hire a salesperson to reach seven figures."

Real Problem (after Reflect & Connect): "I have limiting beliefs about my own potential."

Clear Path (guidance from the Catalyst and Collective): "I need to step into a bigger vision for myself and my business."

MFD: "I am investing in a top-tier salesperson at market rate, and I am committing to being the leader a seven-figure business needs. Starting next week. Period."

Notice what happened after she made her fucking decision:

- Uncertainty ended.
- Energy shifted.
- People aligned.
- Progress started.
- New possibilities emerged.

Why? Because a clear decision, fully committed to, has power that tentative actions never will.

Getting to Your Fucking Decision

The path to your MFD begins with four essential questions, deep inquiries that demand complete honesty with yourself. Start by asking yourself: "What is the real problem?" Not the surface issue you've been telling yourself about. Not the convenient excuse that keeps you comfortable. You're looking for the truth your O-DNA revealed and your connections confirmed. This is the problem beneath the problem, the root cause that keeps showing up in different forms across all aspects of your life or business.

Next, face the question of solution: "What is the clear path forward?" This isn't about finding the perfect answer. It's about identifying a direction that aligns with your reflection, validates through outside perspective, and remains simple enough to act on immediately. The solution must be within your control—no waiting on others, no perfect conditions, no external validation required.

Then comes the crucial question: "What is really stopping me?" This is where brutal honesty becomes essential. Is fear of failure holding you back? The need for absolute certainty? A deep-seated desire to please others? Or perhaps it's simple attachment to comfort—the known devil you prefer to the unknown angel. Name your resistance. Look it in the eye.

Finally, and most importantly: "When will I decide?" Not "soon." Not "when I'm ready." Not "after more research." Set a specific date and time. Write it down. Make it real. Because without a deadline, a decision is just a wish.

The Beautiful Simplicity of Decision

The formula for making your fucking decision is beautifully simple: Name the real problem. Choose your path. Fucking commit to it. That's all it takes—no complicated frameworks, no endless analysis, just clear decision-making followed by purposeful action. You'll know you're ready when you can state the real problem in one clear sentence, when you know in your gut what needs to be done, when you feel that perfect mixture of fear and excitement, and when you're ready to commit despite the uncertainty that remains. This combination of clarity and courage signals your readiness for breakthrough.

Here is the reality you must face: You can reflect forever. You can connect endlessly. You can gather more data, seek more opinions, and analyze more angles. But at some point, somebody needs to Make a Fucking Decision. That somebody is you. The time is now.

Making It Stick

Once you've made your fucking decision, three critical elements will determine its success. First comes immediate action. Within one minute of your decision, you must take a concrete step forward. Create visible momentum. Build early wins. Make your commitment public. The energy of immediate action transforms your decision from a mental exercise into physical reality.

Next, focus on clear communication. Share your decision with key stakeholders—not to seek approval but to declare direction. Set clear expectations about what is changing and why. Define specific metrics for success so everyone knows what winning looks like. Establish accountability structures that keep you moving forward when motivation inevitably wavers.

Finally, maintain unwavering focus. Keep your decision front and center in your daily consciousness. Review it every morning, midday, and every evening before bed. Track your progress religiously. Celebrate small wins that confirm your direction. Your decision isn't a one-time event; it's a daily recommitment to your chosen path. A decision without action is just a thought. A decision without communication is just a secret. A decision without focus is just a moment. But a decision with all three elements becomes unstoppable.

Remember the general from our story? He understood something fundamental about breakthrough: At some point, progress demands decision. The RCD Method ensures that when you reach that decision point, you can then act:

- With clear vision (Reflect)
- With valuable perspective (Connect)
- With committed action (Decide)

This is your moment. Your breakthrough awaits. The only question remaining is: When will you make your fucking decision?

KEY TAKEAWAYS

- **The Power of Decision**
  - Clarity comes through decisive action, not endless analysis.
  - Real decisions end the energy drain of uncertainty.
  - Commitment matters more than perfection.
  - Your breakthrough is waiting on your decision.
- **The MFD Framework Works**
  - Name the real problem with complete honesty.
  - Choose a clear path based on reflection and connection.
  - Commit fully without hedges or escape clauses.
  - Take immediate action to make it real.
- **Success Follows Commitment**
  - Immediate action creates momentum.
  - Clear communication aligns support.
  - Unwavering focus ensures follow-through.
  - Small wins lead to a breakthrough.

REFLECTION QUESTIONS _____

1. About Your Decision

- What decision have you been avoiding?

....

....

- What is the real cost of not deciding?

....

....

- What becomes possible once you decide?

....

....

- What is the worst that could happen if you commit?

....

....

2. About Your Readiness

- Can you state your real problem in one sentence?

....

....

- Do you know what needs to be done?

....

....

- Are you feeling scared but excited?

....

....

- What is still holding you back?

....

....

3. About Your Commitment

- What immediate action will you take?

....

....

- Who needs to know about your decision?

....

....

- How will you measure progress?

....

....

- What support do you need to stay committed?

....

....

....

ACTION STEPS

1. Make Your Fucking Decision

- Set your decision date (within the next seventy-two hours).
- Write out your clear problem statement.
- Define your committed path forward.
- Plan your first twenty-four-hour actions.

....

....

....

....

2. Create Accountability

- Share your decision with key stakeholders.
- Set up progress tracking mechanisms.
- Schedule regular review points.
- Line up necessary support.

....

....

....

....

3. Build Momentum

- Take visible action within twenty-four hours.
- Document your early wins.
- Review your decision daily.
- Celebrate progress milestones.

....

....

....

....

4. Stay Committed

- Keep your decision front and center.
- Review your O-DNA insights regularly.
- Maintain connection with your support system.
- Focus on progress, not perfection.

....

....

....

....

LOOKING AHEAD

The next chapter will explore turning your MFD into a lasting transformation. You'll discover how to make your implementation stick—ensuring that your breakthrough isn't just a moment but a true transformation.

The RCD Method has given you the tools to see clearly, connect powerfully, and decide definitively. It's time to learn how to make those decisions create lasting change.

Are you ready to turn your decision into reality? Turn the page and discover how others used this book to find their hidden truths.

PART THREE

TRANSFORMATION

FOR EVERY COMPLEX
PROBLEM, THERE IS A
SOLUTION WHICH IS CLEAR,
SIMPLE, AND WRONG.

—H. L. Mencken, "Sage of Baltimore"

CHAPTER 7

Real-World Examples

———

IN THIS CHAPTER, WE WILL EXPLORE seven transformative journeys that show how people and organizations moved beyond Blind Blaming and broke free from their obstacles using what you have discovered in this book:

Move from Negativity to Possibility: Stop Blind Blaming and open yourself to new perspectives.

Break Free from the Blame Loop: See the patterns that keep you stuck.

Apply the RCD Method: Use Reflect, Connect, and Decide to create lasting change.

Results: Analyze what happened.

Each case study reveals a different facet of transformation. You'll see how:

- A tech company discovered their marketing problem wasn't about marketing at all.

- A couple's communication issues masked deeper health challenges.

- A fitness enthusiast's weight loss plateau held an unexpected lesson.

- A growing company's turnover crisis revealed a surprising truth.

- A professional's confidence struggle led to an unexpected breakthrough.

- A family's financial stress sparked a complete mindset revolution.

- An industry leader's resistance to change contained a hidden opportunity.

More importantly, you'll learn how to apply these insights to your own obstacles. Through each story, you'll see how the O-DNA framework reveals hidden patterns, how strategic connection provides crucial perspective, and how making a fucking decision transforms possibility into reality.

CASE STUDY 1: WHEN MARKETING ISN'T THE PROBLEM

Initial Situation

Christina's corner office at her software company had boasted floor-to-ceiling windows that framed Seattle's iconic skyline. But the breathtaking view had become invisible to her, obscured by mounting pressure and devastating financials:

- Market share had plummeted from 23 percent to 11 percent in eighteen months.

- The marketing budget had tripled with no positive impact.

- Sales were declining at an accelerating rate.

- Employee surveys showed team morale was at an all-time low.

- The board was getting restless, demanding answers.

Her response was predictable and constant: "If we could just get our marketing message right, everything else would fall into place." Every setback triggered another marketing budget increase, every lost sale sparked another messaging overhaul, and every board meeting became an exercise in defending marketing strategies.

Negativity to Possibility

The turning point came unexpectedly at a local coffee shop. Christina overheard two developers discussing software problems—the exact issues her product was supposed to solve. But they didn't even mention her company as a potential solution. Instead of her usual response—blaming the marketing department or increasing the budget—Christina asked herself a different question: "Is there something else going on?"

This simple shift from blame to curiosity changed everything. She called an emergency executive meeting with one rule: No one could blame marketing. "It was the hardest meeting of my career. Every time we started to drift toward our comfortable marketing discussion, I had to pull us back. I kept asking: 'What if marketing isn't the problem?'"

Breaking Free from the Blame Loop

As the team stopped blaming marketing, they saw their cycle clearly:

1. Lose market share.
2. Blame the marketing message.
3. Increase marketing budget.
4. See no improvement.
5. Lose more market share.
6. Repeat.

This revelation was uncomfortable but liberating. If marketing wasn't the real problem, then what was?

Application of the RCD Method

Reflect: O–DNA Analysis

Christina mapped her obstacle across all five strands:

Health:

- Team exhaustion from constant pivots
- Leadership stress affecting decision-making
- Innovation fatigue setting in

Purpose:
- Mission drift from customer needs
- Value proposition becoming unclear
- Team losing connection to company vision

Relationships:
- Growing disconnect with customers
- Internal silos forming
- Trust eroding between departments

Growth:
- Product evolution stagnating
- Learning from failures blocked by blame
- Innovation culture suffering

Resources:
- Marketing budget draining other areas
- Talent underutilized
- Customer feedback ignored

Through O-DNA, Christina discovered that what looked like a marketing problem was actually a growth obstacle. Their product had stopped evolving while their market transformed. They were solving yesterday's problems with yesterday's solutions.

Connect

Christina shared her O-DNA insights with both her executive coach and her mastermind group. Her coach helped her see how focusing on marketing was actually a way to avoid deeper product issues. Meanwhile, her mastermind group shared similar experiences of mistaking growth problems for marketing problems.

Decide

This led to her MFD (Make a Fucking Decision): "We will be redirecting sixty percent of the marketing budget to product development and reconnecting with our customers' current needs, starting today."

The changes were focused and transformative:

- Established monthly customer advisory board meetings

- Developed three new significant features based on current customer needs

- Retrained sales team to focus on problem-solving rather than feature-selling

- Created direct customer feedback loops

Results

Within six months, the transformation was evident:

- Sales increased 150 percent.
- Marketing costs reduced by 60 percent.
- Team morale scores doubled.
- Customer satisfaction reached all-time highs.

The impact rippled beyond their immediate metrics:

- Engineers reconnected with customer needs.
- Sales team regained confidence.
- Innovation culture reignited.
- The company became known for customer-centric development.

"Our marketing problem was never really about marketing," Christina reflected. "Once we stopped blaming and started seeing, we discovered our real obstacle. We were so busy trying to tell our story better that we had stopped listening to our customers' stories completely."

The breakthrough wasn't about better marketing or bigger budgets. It was about seeing past blame to recognize their growth stagnation. By addressing this one fundamental strand of their obstacle's DNA, everything else began to align.

CASE STUDY 2: BEYOND "JUST TALK IT OUT"

Initial Situation

Amelia stared at the empty side of the bed where David used to sleep, the faint creases on the sheets a reminder of his absence. Three months into their trial separation, their therapist's words still echoed: *You two don't have a communication problem. You have an understanding problem.*

Their situation had become increasingly dire:

- Every conversation ended in conflict.
- Both felt perpetually misunderstood.
- Three marriage counselors had failed to help.
- They were sleeping in separate bedrooms.
- Their ten-year-old had started mediating their conversations.

Their response was always the same: "If we could just learn to talk to each other better, everything would improve." Every argument triggered another communication workshop. Every misunderstanding sparked another attempt at new dialogue techniques. Every therapy session focused on improving their communication skills.

Negativity to Possibility

The turning point came unexpectedly during David's routine physical. Amelia had decided to come along because they had argued that morning over something trivial—David forgetting to confirm dinner plans. By going to his appointment, she sought to better understand what was happening with him.

During the appointment, when David admitted he often felt exhausted no matter how much sleep, had little to no sex drive, and had lost his zest for life. The doctor suggested blood work that revealed low testosterone. Meanwhile, Amelia's casual mention of her stress levels led to her getting an anxiety screening. Instead of blaming communication styles, they faced a new question: "Is there something else going on with our health that is affecting everything else?"

Breaking Free from the Blame Loop

Once they stopped blaming communication, they saw their cycle clearly:

1. Have a conflict.
2. Blame communication styles.
3. Try new communication techniques.
4. See temporary improvement.
5. Fall back into old patterns.
6. Repeat.

This revelation was uncomfortable but necessary. If communication wasn't the real problem, what was it?

The RCD Method

Reflect: O–DNA Analysis

Together, they mapped their obstacle across all five strands:

Health:
- David's chronic fatigue and no sex drive from low testosterone
- Amelia's untreated anxiety
- Both experiencing mood swings
- Sleep deprivation affecting judgment
- Stress manifesting physically

Purpose:
- Losing sight of shared dreams
- Individual goals diverging
- Missing sense of partnership
- Forgetting why they chose each other
- Values feeling misaligned

Relationships:
- Growing emotional distance
- Children feeling stressed
- Extended family concerns

- Social isolation increasing
- Professional impacts showing

Growth:
- Personal development stalled
- Avoiding challenges together
- Learning blocked by defensiveness
- Missing opportunities for connection
- Fear limiting possibilities

Resources:
- Energy constantly depleted
- Time spent on wrong solutions
- Emotional reserves exhausted
- Support systems underutilized
- Financial strain from multiple therapists

Through O-DNA, they discovered that their communication problem was actually a health obstacle expressing itself through their interactions. Their physical and mental health challenges were creating a perfect storm of misunderstanding.

Connect

The doctor reviewed David's blood work results and informed him that he had low testosterone and recommended pellets that would reverse the issue two weeks after the procedure. They also joined a support group for couples, where they found others facing similar challenges. Their therapist helped them see how anxiety and other health issues were affecting their relationship dynamics.

Decide

This led to their MFD (Make a Fucking Decision): "We are treating our health issues first. Everything else is second, starting today."

The changes were focused but transformative:

- David started Low-T treatment with pellets.
- Amelia began anxiety management therapy.
- They developed communication protocols around energy levels.
- They established health-conscious check-ins.

Results

Within three months, the transformation was evident:

- Arguments decreased by 80 percent.
- Both felt understood and appreciated.
- They returned to sharing a bedroom.
- Intimacy and connection deepened.
- They started enjoying each other again.

The impact rippled beyond their marriage:

- Their children became more emotionally expressive and less stressed.
- Family dinner conversations transformed.
- The home atmosphere shifted from tension to connection.
- Their story inspired others to seek medical help.
- They started a support group for couples.

"All that time, we both thought we were fighting about communication," Amelia said. "In reality, we were fighting against ourselves. Once we addressed our health issues—my anxiety, his low testosterone—we could finally hear each other."

The breakthrough wasn't about better communication techniques or more therapy. It was about seeing past blame to recognize their health challenges. By addressing this one fundamental strand of their O-DNA, everything else began to heal.

CASE STUDY 3: WHEN INTENSITY ISN'T THE ANSWER

Initial Situation

Carrie stepped off the treadmill for what she promised would be the last time. After ten years of intense workouts, countless personal training sessions, and enough fitness apps to fill her phone, the numbers hadn't budged. At age thirty-eight, she had begun to accept her athletic plateau.

Her situation was frustratingly familiar:

- Completed multiple high-intensity training programs
- Spent over $15,000 on various fitness solutions
- Maintained an intense workout schedule with minimal results
- Tracked every rep and set with obsessive precision
- Experienced increasing fitness anxiety and frustration
- Dealt with multiple injuries that caused issues with her consistency

Her response was always the same: "If I could just push harder in my workouts, I would finally see results." Every failed attempt triggered another extreme training program. Every pound gained sparked another intense exercise challenge. Every setback reinforced her belief that she simply wasn't working hard enough.

Negativity to Possibility

The turning point came during a conversation with Betty, a fitness researcher at her local gym. Watching Carrie complete another intense CrossFit session, Betty noticed something wasn't adding up: Someone this dedicated should be seeing results.

"I notice you're here every day, pushing yourself to the limit," Betty said. "You are one of the most committed people I know. But something about your approach doesn't make sense. You work out intensely, you're careful about form, yet you're not seeing the results you expect." Instead of her usual pattern of blaming herself and her lack of intensity, Carrie faced a new question: "Is there something fundamental missing from my fitness routine?"

Breaking Free from the Blame Loop

Once she stopped blaming workout intensity, she saw her cycle clearly:

1. Results don't change.
2. Blame lack of effort.
3. Increase workout intensity.
4. Follow stricter programs.
5. See worse results.
6. Repeat.

This revelation was uncomfortable but liberating. If intensity wasn't the real problem, then what was it?

The RCD Method

Reflect: O-DNA Analysis

Carrie mapped her obstacle across all five strands:

Health:
- Extreme fatigue despite intense workouts
- Joint pain after training sessions
- Recovery taking longer than usual
- Decreased daily movement outside gym
- Persistent muscle soreness

Purpose:
- Identity tied to workout intensity
- Self-worth connected to gym performance
- Missing daily joyful movements
- Lost connection with natural rhythm
- Exercise feeling punishment-based

Relationships:

- Avoiding walking with friends
- Family activities becoming workout-focused
- Partner feeling neglected
- Professional impact from fatigue
- Social life revolving around gym

Growth:

- Fixed mindset about exercise
- Resistance to low-intensity movement
- Fear of "wasting time" walking
- Avoiding lifestyle changes
- Stuck in high-intensity mindset

Resources:

- Time consumed by gym sessions
- Money wasted on extreme programs
- Energy depleted from overtraining
- Natural movement opportunities missed
- Daily activity potential untapped

Reflect

Through O-DNA, Carrie discovered her intensity problem was actually a fundamental misunderstanding of movement principles requiring a complete routine overhaul.

Connect

Her coach helped her see the patterns in her O-DNA, particularly how her focus on intense workouts had led to neglecting basic movement patterns. Her fitness community included several athletes who shared similar experiences, leading her to research on NEAT (Non-Exercise Activity Thermogenesis).

Decide

This led to her MFD (Make a Fucking Decision): "I'm treating this as a movement issue, not an intensity problem, starting today."

The changes were focused but transformative:

- Implemented 10,000 daily steps goal
- Reduced high-intensity sessions
- Developed a balanced movement plan
- Created opportunities for natural movement

Results

Within six months, the transformation was evident:

- She lost twenty-five pounds without extreme workouts.
- Energy levels stabilized throughout day.
- Recovery time improved dramatically.
- Movement became enjoyable again.
- Overall fitness markers improved.
- Daily activity became sustainable.

The impact rippled beyond her fitness:

- Her husband joined her on evening walks.
- Family activities became movement-focused.
- Her colleagues started a lunch walking group.
- She started a movement-first fitness community.
- Developed a program for over-trained athletes.

"The irony," Carrie reflected, "is that I have spent years forcing my body when what I needed was to move it naturally. Once I understood what was happening, the solution became clear. It wasn't about pushing harder. It was about moving smarter."

The breakthrough wasn't about more intensity or stricter programs. It was about seeing past the gym to recognize her body's actual needs. By addressing this one fundamental strand of her obstacle's DNA, everything else began to align.

CASE STUDY 4: WHEN LOYALTY ISN'T THE ISSUE

Initial Situation

Tom stood at the window of his corner office at his AI company, watching another talented employee walk to their car, laptop box tucked under one arm. He was the fifth senior developer to quit in three months. As CEO of the fastest-growing tech company in Austin, he should have been celebrating their 300 percent year-over-year growth. Instead, he felt a hollow ache in his chest.

The situation was paradoxical:

- Employee turnover reached 40 percent annually.
- Recruitment costs exceeded $2 million.
- Project deadlines consistently slipped.
- Customer support quality declined.
- Company culture surveys showed alarming results.

Yet on paper they were thriving:

- Revenue had tripled in eighteen months.
- Customer base had grown from 100 to 1,500.
- Staff size had expanded from 50 to 200.
- Industry recognition and awards poured in.

His response to the executive team was always the same: "If they were just more loyal, we wouldn't have these issues." Every departure triggered another rant about millennials, and every missed deadline sparked another complaint about the "job-hopping" mentality.

Negativity to Possibility

The wake-up call came during a critical board meeting. Their lead investor leaned forward and asked, "What's the real cost of your turnover problem?" The room fell silent when the CFO finally calculated $4.2

million annually. Instead of his usual pattern of blaming generational attitudes, Tom faced a new question: "Is there something else going on beneath our turnover numbers?"

Breaking Free from the Blame Loop

Once he stopped blaming the workforce, he saw the cycle clearly:

1. Lose talented people.
2. Blame generational attitudes.
3. Make superficial changes.
4. See more departures.
5. Increase recruitment efforts.
6. Repeat.

This revelation was uncomfortable but necessary. If loyalty wasn't the real problem, then what was it?

The RCD Method

Reflect: O-DNA Analysis

Tom mapped the obstacle across all five strands:

Health:

- Burnout becoming normalized
- Stress-related sick days increasing
- Mental health concerns rising
- Work-life boundaries eroding
- Team energy depleting

Purpose:

- Mission disconnect growing
- Values feeling hollow
- Career paths unclear
- Impact not visible
- Personal growth stagnating

Relationships:

- Manager-team trust breaking down
- Cross-team collaboration suffering
- Mentorship lacking
- Communication channels blocked
- Recognition systems failing

Growth:

- Leadership development missing
- Skill-building opportunities limited
- Feedback systems broken
- Innovation stifled
- Learning culture absent

Resources:

- Training budgets underutilized
- Time for development scarce
- Knowledge transfer breaking down
- Support systems inadequate
- Tools and systems outdated

Through O-DNA, Tom discovered their "loyalty problem" was actually a growth obstacle. The company had invested in expansion but neglected development.

Connect

His executive coach helped him see how blaming generational differences masked systemic issues. His mastermind group of other tech CEOs shared similar experiences and solutions for building strong development cultures.

Decide

This led to his MFD (Make a Fucking Decision): "We are building a Leadership Academy and clear career frameworks, starting next month."

The changes were focused but transformative:

- Created comprehensive management training
- Established clear career progression paths
- Implemented new feedback systems
- Rebuilt company values from the ground up
- Invested in personal development programs

Results

Within months, the transformation was evident:

- Annual turnover dropped from 40 percent to 14 percent.
- Employee satisfaction scores doubled.
- Productivity rose by 40 percent.
- Recruitment expenses dropped 65 percent.
- Project delivery times improved by 30 percent.

The impact rippled beyond their organization:

- The Leadership Academy set industry standards.
- Cross-department collaboration thrived.
- Stable teams fueled greater innovation.
- Their frameworks inspired other companies.
- Business journals featured their success.

"We thought we had a loyalty problem when we actually had a growth problem," Tom admitted. "Once we stopped blaming millennials and started investing in our people's development, everything changed. Loyalty isn't something you demand; it's something you earn by helping people grow."

The breakthrough wasn't about finding more loyal employees or blaming generational differences. It was about seeing past blame to recognize their growth and development gaps. By addressing this one fundamental strand of their obstacle's DNA, everything else began to align.

CASE STUDY 5: WHEN CONFIDENCE ISN'T THE ANSWER

Initial Situation

Kim sat in her parked car outside her office, gripping the steering wheel as she rehearsed the presentation she'd never give. Her laptop displayed the slides she had spent countless late nights perfecting. For the third time this quarter, she had poured her energy into writing a brilliant proposal, only to watch silently as someone else—someone with less innovative ideas and less effort invested—took the spotlight.

On paper, her life looked enviably organized:

- Senior analyst position at a respected consulting firm
- Master's degree from a top university
- Stable long-term relationship
- Active social circle
- Comfortable financial situation

But beneath the polished surface:

- Chronic self-doubt paralyzed her decision-making.
- Brilliant ideas went unshared in meetings.
- She was passed over for promotions despite superior work.
- Her anxiety about social interactions was increasing.
- Her personal relationships were becoming superficial.
- Insomnia and stress-related health issues were rapidly emerging.

Her response was always the same: "If I could just get everything perfect—every detail, every word, every outcome—then maybe I'd finally feel confident enough to speak up." Every meeting triggered another round of relentless over-preparation. Every presentation sparked an exhausting cycle of perfectionism.

Negativity to Possibility

The turning point came during a company retreat when a junior colleague tearfully admitted to feeling intimidated by Kim's "perfect, put-together image." Kim was stunned. Instead of her usual pattern of seeking more perfection, she faced a new question: "Is there something else going on beneath my need for perfection?"

Breaking Free from the Blame Loop

Once she stopped blaming her lack of confidence, she saw her cycle clearly:

1. Feel insecure.
2. Seek perfection.
3. Overprepare.
4. Remain silent.
5. Miss opportunities.
6. Repeat.

This revelation was uncomfortable but liberating. If confidence wasn't the real problem, what was it?

The RCD Method

Reflect: O–DNA Analysis

Kim mapped her obstacle across all five strands:

Health:

- Chronic anxiety manifesting physically
- Sleep disrupted by perfectionism
- Stress-induced health issues
- Energy depleted by over-preparation
- Physical symptoms of fear

Purpose:

- True voice silenced by fear
- Impact limited by perfectionism

- Values compromised for appearance
- Mission unclear beneath performance
- Authenticity sacrificed for image

Relationships:

- Genuine connections blocked
- Others kept at safe distance
- Surface-level interactions only
- Fear of vulnerability dominant
- Support systems underutilized

Growth:

- Learning limited by fear of mistakes
- Feedback avoided to maintain image
- Development stalled by perfectionism
- Opportunities missed through silence
- Comfort zone becoming a prison

Resources:

- Time wasted on overpreparation
- Energy drained by performance
- Natural talents suppressed
- Network connections superficial
- Support available but unused

Through O-DNA, Kim discovered her confidence problem was actually a relationship obstacle. Her perfectionism had become a barrier to genuine connection—with others and herself.

Connect

Her coach helped her see how perfectionism was a shield against vulnerability. Her mastermind group provided a safe space to practice being imperfect, showing her that authentic connection was more powerful than perfect performance.

Decide

This led to her MFD (Make a Fucking Decision): "I am choosing authentic connection over perfect performance, starting today."

The changes were focused but transformative:

- She became committed to speaking up in every meeting.
- She started mentoring junior colleagues.
- She joined Toastmasters.
- She shared her journey openly with her team.
- She practiced intentional imperfection.

Results

Within six months, the transformation was evident:

- She was promoted to Team Lead.
- Her speaking anxiety reduced by 70 percent.
- Her sleep quality improved dramatically.
- She launched a successful mentoring program.
- She built deeper, meaningful relationships.

The impact rippled beyond her career:

- Team innovation flourished through psychological safety.
- Communication improved across departments.
- More women found their voice through her leadership.
- A women's leadership network was created.
- She helped cultivate a culture of authenticity.

"I thought perfection was the key to mattering," Kim admitted. "I spent years meticulously curating every word and move, thinking that would make me worthy. Turns out, people connect with authenticity, not perfection. The moment I stopped trying to be perfect, I started having a real impact at work."

The breakthrough wasn't about building more confidence or achieving perfection. It was about seeing past blame to recognize how perfectionism blocked genuine connection. By addressing this one fundamental strand of her obstacle's DNA, everything else began to align.

CASE STUDY 6: WHEN MAKING MORE ISN'T THE ANSWER

Initial Situation

Anthony sat hunched over his kitchen table, credit card statements spread like a battlefield before him. At age forty-five, his life looked like a picture of success from the outside—a six-figure salary as a software engineer, a comfortable home in a nice neighborhood, and two kids thriving in private school.

On paper, his life looked impressive:

- Annual income of $175,000
- Beautiful $750,000 home in Seattle
- Two children in top-rated private schools
- Luxury car lease
- Regular family vacations
- Active social life

But the reality was crushing:

- $87,000 in credit card debt across six cards
- No emergency savings
- Minimal retirement contributions
- Monthly expenses exceeding income
- Growing anxiety about money
- Hiding financial struggles from family

Anthony's response was always the same: "If I could just make more money, everything would work itself out." Every unexpected expense triggered another side hustle. Every bill sparked a new job search. Every month ended with promises that next month would be different.

Negativity to Possibility

The wake-up call came during his daughter's college planning meeting.

As the counselor discussed tuition options and asked about their 529 plan, Tom felt a cold sweat break out. Instead of his usual pattern of blaming his income, he faced a new question: "Is there something else going on with my relationship with money?"

Breaking Free from the Blame Loop

Once he stopped blaming insufficient income, he saw his cycle clearly:

1. Face financial pressure.
2. Blame income level.
3. Seek more income.
4. Increase spending.
5. Face more pressure.
6. Repeat.

This revelation was uncomfortable but necessary. If income wasn't the real problem, then what was?

The RCD Method

Reflect: O-DNA Analysis

Anthony mapped his obstacle across all five strands:

Health:

- Sleep disrupted by money anxiety
- Stress affecting eating habits
- Physical symptoms of worry
- Energy depleted by side hustles
- Chronic tension headaches

Purpose:

- Money decisions disconnected from values
- Spending to fill emotional voids
- Status driving financial choices
- Missing sense of financial purpose
- Legacy concerns unaddressed

Relationships:
- Financial secrets straining marriage
- Kids sensing money tension
- Social spending creating pressure
- Professional relationships affected
- Support systems avoided

Growth:
- Fixed mindset about wealth
- Avoiding financial education
- Resistance to lifestyle changes
- Learning blocked by shame
- Fear limiting options

Resources:
- Income poorly aligned with values
- Time wasted on temporary fixes
- Energy scattered across side hustles
- Support systems underutilized
- Financial tools misunderstood

Through O-DNA, Anthony discovered his money problem was actually a purpose obstacle. His financial decisions were not aligned with his true values and goals.

Connect

His financial coach helped him see how his childhood experiences with scarcity shaped his current money patterns. His mastermind group shared similar struggles and solutions, showing him new possibilities for aligning money with meaning.

Decide

This led to his MFD (Make a Fucking Decision): "We are completely resetting our relationship with money as a family, starting today."

The changes were focused but transformative:

- He downsized his home and car to reduce expenses.
- He adopted zero-based budgeting.
- He established complete financial transparency.
- He started teaching his kids financial literacy.
- He aligned his spending with family values.

Results

Within eighteen months, the transformation was evident:

- Eliminated credit card debt completely
- Built $30,000 emergency fund
- Increased retirement contributions to 15 percent
- Cut monthly expenses by 40 percent
- Improved credit score by 150 points

The impact rippled beyond their finances:

- His children developed healthy money habits.
- His marriage strengthened through transparency.
- His family discussions became more authentic.
- He started a financial wellness blog.
- He began leading community workshops on money mindset.

"I thought making more money would solve everything," Anthony said. "But once we aligned our spending with our values and started being honest about money, we discovered we already had enough. It wasn't about earning more; it was about living with purpose."

The breakthrough wasn't about budgeting apps or cutting expenses. It was about seeing past blame to recognize the misalignment between money and meaning. By addressing this one fundamental strand of their obstacle's DNA, everything else began to align.

CASE STUDY 7: WHEN TRADITION ISN'T THE ANSWER

Initial Situation

NOTE: The following case study features an experience shared by a studio executive I recently discovered. They've launched a new studio built on a fascinating business model that is currently thriving. The story offers valuable insights worth sharing!

Michael sat alone in his darkened screening room, watching another box office projection slide deeper into the red. As head of production for over two decades, he had been the studio's guardian, keeping the lights on with tried-and-true blockbuster formulas. But now, his once-unshakable playbook felt like a relic.

The surface metrics looked solid:

- $2 billion annual production budget
- Strong partnerships with top-tier talent
- Rich library of valuable intellectual property
- Seasoned executive team
- Prestigious industry reputation

But beneath the surface:

- Box office returns declining 30 percent year-over-year
- Streaming services outbidding for talent
- Young audiences shifting to digital platforms
- Production costs spiraling upward
- Development pipeline growing stagnant

His response was always the same: "Streaming is just a fad. People will always want the theatrical experience." Every disappointing opening weekend triggered another passionate defense of traditional cinema. Every streaming success was dismissed as temporary.

Negativity to Possibility

The wake-up call came during a board meeting when his teenage daughter, visiting for Take Your Child to Work Day, innocently asked, "Dad, why doesn't anyone I know go to movies anymore?" Instead of his usual pattern of dismissing changing viewer habits or fatigue, Michael faced a new question: "Is there something else going on besides audience preferences?"

Breaking Free from the Blame Loop

Once he stopped blaming industry disruption, he saw his cycle clearly:
1. Box office numbers drop.
2. Blame streaming services.
3. Double down on traditional methods.
4. Lose more audience share.
5. Defend outdated models resolutely.
6. Repeat.

This revelation was uncomfortable but necessary. If market disruption wasn't the real problem, then what was?

The RCD Method

Reflect: O–DNA Analysis

Michael mapped his obstacle across all five strands:

Health:
- Organizational stress at all-time high
- Creative energy stagnating
- Innovation fatigue setting in
- Decision paralysis growing
- Resistance creating tension

Purpose:
- Mission disconnect with new audiences
- Core values becoming outdated

- Impact diminishing
- Story relevance fading
- Cultural connection weakening

Relationships:

- Young talent choosing competitors
- Audience connection breaking down
- Partner relationships straining
- Team trust eroding
- Industry position weakening

Growth:

- Learning blocked by bias
- Innovation resisted
- Change viewed as threat
- Adaptation avoided
- Development stalled

Resources:

- Traditional investments failing
- Digital capabilities lacking
- Talent choosing competitors
- Technology falling behind
- Market share shrinking

Through O-DNA, Michael discovered their disruption problem was actually a growth obstacle. Their resistance to change was not protecting the business; it was preventing evolution.

Connect

His executive coach helped him see how fear of irrelevance was driving resistance. His mastermind group shared similar experiences of transforming traditional businesses for the digital age.

Decide

This led to his MFD (Make a Fucking Decision): "Today marks the beginning of our journey as a multi-platform entertainment powerhouse."

The changes were focused but transformative:

- Created hybrid release strategy
- Invested in virtual production
- Established digital-first division
- Built a recurring income model for releases
- Committed to listening to feedback from consumers

Results

Within months, the transformation was evident:

- Overall revenue surged by 50 percent.
- Digital revenue grew by 200 percent.
- Production costs dropped by 25 percent.
- Market share in streaming doubled.
- Young audience engagement increased by 80 percent.

The impact rippled beyond their studio:

- Industry adoption of hybrid models accelerated.
- Cross-platform storytelling evolved.
- New talent attracted to innovative approach.
- Traditional theaters embraced change.
- Entertainment ecosystem transformed.

"I thought I was protecting the magic of cinema," Michael said. "But what makes storytelling magical isn't the platform. It's the connection with audiences. Once we stopped fighting change and started embracing growth, we found new ways to create that magic."

The breakthrough wasn't about choosing between traditional and new media. It was about seeing past blame to recognize their resistance to growth and evolution. By addressing this one fundamental strand of their O-DNA, everything else began to align.

KEY INSIGHTS FROM THE TRANSFORMATIONS

Pattern Recognition Across Stories

1. The Power of O-DNA Analysis
   - Each breakthrough started with identifying the true obstacle strand.
   - Christina's marketing issues revealed a growth challenge.
   - Amelia and David's communication problems masked health issues.
   - Carrie's weight plateau concealed hormonal imbalances.
   - Tom's loyalty concerns revealed development gaps.
   - Kim's confidence struggles stemmed from relationship barriers.
   - Anthony's income focus masked purpose misalignment.
   - Michael's resistance to change blocked organizational growth.

2. The Breakthrough Process
   - Moving from blame to curiosity opened new possibilities.
   - Breaking free from established blame loops revealed true patterns.
   - Strategic connection provided crucial outside perspective.
   - Making a fucking decision (MFD) transformed insight into action.

3. The Results
   - Individual breakthroughs created organizational transformation.
   - Personal insights led to systemic changes.
   - Solutions in one area catalyzed improvements across all strands.
   - Initial changes sparked wider industry impact.

REFLECTION QUESTIONS

Understanding Your Obstacle

1. Pattern Recognition

   - What recurring explanations do you give for your current challenges?

   ....

   ....

   - Which strand of O-DNA feels most relevant to your situation?

   ....

   ....

   - What cycles of blame can you identify in your approach?

   ....

   ....

2. Hidden Connections

   - Like Amelia and David's health issues, what underlying factors might you be missing?

   ....

   ....

   - Similar to Christina's marketing focus, are you potentially solving the wrong problem?

   ....

   ....

   ....

- What assumptions, like Tom's views on loyalty, might be limiting your perspective?

....

....

3. Growth Opportunities

- What outside perspectives, like Carrie's trainer, might offer new insights?

....

....

- How might your obstacle, like Kim's perfectionism, actually protect you from something deeper?

....

....

- What values or purposes, like Anthony's financial decisions, might need realignment?

....

....

ACTION STEPS

Creating Your Breakthrough

1. Conduct Your O-DNA Analysis

- Map your obstacle across all five strands.
- Document recurring patterns and cycles.
- Identify potential blind spots and assumptions.
- Note areas where outside perspective might help.

....

....

....

....

2. Build Your Support System

- Identify potential mentors or advisors.
- Research relevant professional support.
- Consider joining or forming a mastermind group.
- Plan regular check-ins and accountability structures.

....

....

....

....

....

3. Prepare for Your MFD (Make a Fucking Decision)

- Set a specific date for your decision.
- Define clear, measurable outcomes.
- Create an implementation timeline.
- Establish accountability measures.

....

....

....

....

....

LOOKING AHEAD

These seven stories illustrate a fundamental truth about meaningful change: Breakthroughs happen when we shift from surface-level solutions to systemic understanding. Whether it was David discovering his hormone imbalance, Carrie realizing the power of daily movement, or the other transformative journeys shared, each breakthrough began with challenging deeply held assumptions. Through the RCD Method—Reflect, Connect, Decide—these individuals not only solved problems, they transformed their entire approach to obstacles, creating ripple effects that extended far beyond their initial challenges.

The path to lasting change is systematic, not linear. Success demands thoughtful implementation, strategic connection, and environmental redesign. Having the initial motivation won't cut it. As you apply these lessons to your own challenges, remember that true transformation requires building sustainable systems, creating supportive networks, and maintaining the courage to question your fundamental assumptions about what is possible. There are no quick fixes.

Your breakthrough journey begins with recognizing patterns, then grows through strategic connection, and culminates in decisive action that reshapes not just your immediate challenge, but your entire approach to obstacle navigation.

YOUR CALL TO ACTION

As we close this chapter, remember that every person in these case studies started precisely where you are—stuck, frustrated, and convinced they knew what their obstacle was. Their breakthrough began when they used O-DNA to discover what was holding them back.

Your breakthrough is inevitable when you find the right strand. The only question is: Are you ready to make your fucking decision?

Turn the page, and let's begin your implementation journey.

Beyond Blind Blaming:
Your Path Forward

———

L ATE ONE EVENING, I SAT ALONE IN MY OFFICE, the warm glow of a desk lamp cutting through the darkness and casting long shadows across the room. In my hand, I held an old, scuffed baseball, its leather worn smooth from years of handling. As I turned it over in my fingers, its weight grounded me in a flood of memories. That baseball represented a piece of my story, a relic from when life felt impossibly vast and frustratingly small.

I was reminded of that younger version of myself, standing awkwardly on a dusty baseball field, gripping a bat far too tightly. The cheers and advice of well-meaning adults swirled around me like a confusing storm.

"Keep your eye on the ball!" they'd shouted. But how could I? No one realized I literally couldn't see the ball. To them, it was a matter of effort, coordination, or willingness to try harder or practice more. They blamed everything—except my vision.

I still feel the sting of those moments because no one cared to identify the real problem. Isn't that how life often works? Obstacles surround us, yet we spend so much time blaming the wrong things. We focus on the surface—what's visible, what seems obvious—while the true source of our struggles hides beneath, unseen and untouched, like the ball I couldn't easily see.

That baseball is not only a reminder of my boyhood but a symbol of something universal. We all, at some point, misdiagnose the very things holding us back. We blind ourselves to the real O-DNA of our challenges, chasing easy answers and quick fixes. How often do we blame circumstances, others, or even ourselves without asking if we're focusing on the wrong thing?

As I look at that baseball, I think about everything we've explored in this book. We've discussed how **Blind Blaming** keeps us trapped in cycles of frustration, spinning our wheels without progress. We've examined the **Blame Loop**, where finger-pointing, helplessness, and our inability to see solutions repeat endlessly. Most importantly, we've introduced the **RCD Method**, a powerful framework to help you break free from these patterns. By redefining your challenges, you can create breakthroughs and uncover the deeper truths of what it means to be human.

The Journey Ahead

The elegance of this approach lies in its application to any breakthrough journey. We've all stood on our version of that dusty baseball field, feeling stuck, misunderstood, or unseen. But here's what I hope you take away: *You are not alone in this.* Your struggles have meaning, and within that meaning lies power. Obstacles are challenges to endure and opportunities to grow, shift your perspective, and rewrite your story. This journey isn't just mine; it's ours. The tools are available, waiting for you to pick them up and build something new.

Will you step up to the plate and swing for the fences?

THE HIDDEN TRUTH REVEALED

Remember the core insight that started our journey: *You are not failing at solving your problems. You are succeeding perfectly at solving the wrong ones.* This realization changes everything. Our journey revealed three crucial strategies that transform how we approach our challenges:

1. **Moving from Negativity to Possibility**: When we stop blaming and complaining, we create space to see what's there. This first step allows us to look beyond our assumptions as if we were taking off a blindfold.

2. **Breaking Free to See**: Escaping the Blame Loop isn't just about changing behavior and recognizing patterns. When we break free, we can finally see our situation.

3. **Using the RCD Method**: This final step combines three powerful elements:

   ■ Reflect: Use O-DNA to understand your obstacle's actual DNA.

   ■ Connect: Engage with others to gain perspective and insight.

   ■ Decide: Make a Fucking Decision (MFD) to move forward.

YOUR JOURNEY FORWARD

As you begin your journey beyond Blind Blaming, remember this: Every breakthrough starts with truly understanding what is holding you back. Through O-DNA, you'll dive into these possible categories:

■ Health: Your physical and mental well-being patterns
■ Purpose: Your mission and values alignment
■ Growth: Your learning and development edges
■ Relationships: Your connection and support networks
■ Resources: Your time, energy, and asset flows

But understanding alone isn't enough. You need to:

■ Connect with others who can help you see what you might miss.
■ Make a Fucking Decision when the path becomes clear.
■ Take action despite uncertainty.

THE FINAL TRUTH

Here is what I want you to take away from our journey together: Your obstacles are not random. They have specific DNA unique to you, which you can understand through reflection and self-awareness. These challenges are not just there to trip you up; they hold lessons and insights that, once uncovered, can help you move forward. Your blind spots, the areas you can't see on your own, become visible through connection— with others, mentors, and people who can offer a different perspective.

Your breakthrough, the moment everything changes, happens when you finally Make a Fucking Decision to do something. Not when you're stuck overthinking or waiting for the "right time," but when you act with clarity and courage.

Life is too short to stay trapped in patterns that no longer serve you, no matter how familiar or comfortable they might feel. Don't let Blind Blaming or excuses keep you from seeing the true nature of your obstacles. Look deeper, ask questions, and own your role in the process. Your future is too important to be left to chance or a clouded vision. You have the power to create the change you want, but it starts with understanding what is holding you back and deciding to move forward. Your breakthrough awaits. The only question is: Are you ready to move beyond Blind Blaming and step into transformation?

Remember that baseball on my desk? It reminds me daily that our most significant breakthroughs often come not from trying harder but from seeing clearer, connecting authentically, and deciding bravely.

Your journey beyond Blind Blaming starts now.

Make your fucking decision.

Take action.

Your breakthrough awaits.

Notes

————

Chapter 1: Understanding Blind Blaming

1. Ross, L. (1977). "The intuitive psychologist and his shortcomings." *Advances in Experimental Social Psychology*, 10, 173–220.

2. Amy C. Edmondson, *The Fearless Organization: Creating Psychological Safety in the Workplace for Learning*, Wiley; 1st edition (November 20, 2018).

3. Learning Disabilities Association of America. (n.d.). New to LD. Retrieved from https://ldaamerica.org/support/new-to-ld/.

4. Matthew Walker, *Why We Sleep: Unlocking the Power of Sleep and Dreams*. Scribner; Illustrated edition (October 3, 2017).

5. Matthew Dixon, *The Effortless Experience: Conquering the New Battleground for Customer Loyalty*, Portfolio Penguin (September 26, 2013).

6. Kahneman, D., & Tversky, A. (1973). "Availability: A heuristic for judging frequency and probability." *Cognitive Psychology*, 5(2), 207–232.

7. Nickerson, R. S. (1998). "Confirmation bias: A ubiquitous phenomenon in many guises." *Review of General Psychology*, 2(2), 175–220.

8. Langer, E. J. (1975). "The Illusion of Control," *Journal of Personality and Social Psychology*, 32(2), 311–328. https://doi.org/10.1037/0022-3514.32.2.311.

9. Wason, P. C. (1960). "On the failure to eliminate hypotheses in a conceptual task." *Quarterly Journal of Experimental Psychology*, 12(3), 129–140.

10. Miller, D. T., & Ross, M. (1975). "Self-serving biases in the attribution of causality: Fact or fiction?" *Psychological Bulletin*, 82(2), 213–225.

11. Carol S. Dweck, *Mindset: The New Psychology of Success*. Random House (February 28, 2006).

12. Baumeister, R. F., *Self-Regulation and Self-Control: Selected Works*, Routledge 2018.

13. Merkel DL. "Youth sport: positive and negative impact on young athletes." Open Access *J Sports Med*. 2013 May 31;4:151–60. doi: 10.2147/OAJSM. S33556. PMID: 24379720; PMCID: PMC3871410.

14. Sun TY, Hardin J, Nieva HR, Natarajan K, Cheng RF, Ryan P, Elhadad N. "Large-scale characterization of gender differences in diagnosis prevalence and time to diagnosis." *medRxiv* [Preprint]. 2023 Oct 16:2023.10.12.23296976. doi: 10.1101/2023.10.12.23296976. PMID: 37873224; PMCID: PMC10592987.

15. Rosecká N, Machek O. "How Relational Conflict Harms Family Firm Performance: The Mediating Role of Family Social Capital and the Moderating Role of Family Ownership." *J Fam Econ Issues*. 2022 Dec 10:1–16. doi: 10.1007/s10834-022-09877-6. Epub ahead of print. PMID: 36533122; PMCID: PMC9739348.

16. Donaldson, W. (2024). "FAMILY and FAMILY BUSINESS INTERSECTIONS, FAILURE MODES, and RECOMMENDATIONS." *Small Business Institute Journal*, 20(1), 20–25. https://doi.org/10.53703/001c.115385Jensen, M. C. (1993). The modern industrial revolution, exit, and the failure of internal control systems. The Journal of Finance, 48(3), 831. https://doi.org/10.2307/2329018.

Chapter 2: Negativity to Possibility

1. Jack Canfield, *The Success Principles: How to Get from Where You Are to Where You Want to Be*, Mariner Books; Anniversary edition (March 18, 2025).

2. Jocko Willink and Leif Babin, *Extreme Ownership: How U.S. Navy Seals Lead and Win*, St. Martin's Press; 1st edition (November 21, 2017).

3. Morey JN, Boggero IA, Scott AB, Segerstrom SC. "Current Directions in Stress and Human Immune Function." *Curr Opin Psychol*. 2015 Oct 1;5:13–17. doi: 10.1016/j.copsyc.2015.03.007. PMID: 26086030; PMCID: PMC4465119.

Chapter 3: The Blame Loop Revealed

1. Daniel Kahneman, *Thinking, Fast and Slow*. Farrar, Straus and Giroux; 1st edition (October 25, 2011).

2. Steven Covey, *The 7 Habits of Highly Effective People: Powerful Lessons in Personal Change* (New York, NY: Simon & Schuster).

3. Loudon I. Ignaz Phillip "Semmelweis' studies of death in childbirth." *J R Soc Med.* 2013 Nov;106(11):461–3. doi: 10.1177/0141076813507844. PMID: 24158918; PMCID: PMC3807776.

4. Peter M. Senge, *The Fifth Discipline: The Art and Practice of the Learning Organization*, Doubleday; Revised & Updated edition (March 21, 2006).

5. McLuhan, M. (n.d.) quote, BrainyQuote 2025, https://brainly.com/question/49320545.

6. Albert Einstein quote, BrainyQuote 2025, https://www.brainyquote.com/quotes/albert_einstein_121993.

7. Chris Argyris, *Overcoming Organizational Defenses: Facilitating Organizational Learning.* Pearson; 1st edition (March 15, 1990).

8. Christensen, Clayton M. *The Innovator's Dilemma: When New Technologies Cause Great Firms to Fail.* Boston, MA: Harvard Business School Press, 1997.

9. Joel Barker, *Paradigms: The Business of Discovering the Future* (New York, NY, HarperBusiness 1993).

10. Immanuel Kant, *Critique of Pure Reason.* (N. K. Smith, Trans. Macmillan Publishing Company (1781/1998).

11. Joel Barker, *Paradigms.*

Chapter 4: Discover the Hidden Truth

1. Carol. S. Dweck, *Mindset.*

2. Mark Nevins, "How To Get Stuff Done: The Eisenhower Matrix (a.k.a. The Urgent Vs. the Important)," January 5, 2023,

    https://www.forbes.com/sites/hillennevins/2023/01/05/how-to-get-stuff-done-the-eisenhower-matrix-aka-the-urgent-vs-the-important/.

Chapter 5: Connect: Share Your Discovery

1. Napoleon Hill, *Think and Grow Rich.* (Rev. ed. Greenwich, Conn., Fawcett Publications, 1963).

Chapter 6: Turn Insight into Action

1. Feldman G, Lian H, Kosinski M, Stillwell D. Frankly, We Do Give a Damn: The Relationship Between Profanity and Honesty. Soc Psychol Personal Sci. 2017 Sep;8(7):816-826. doi: 10.1177/1948550616681055. Epub 2017 Jan 15. PMID: 29187959; PMCID: PMC5686790.

Resources

———

HAVE A SUCCESS STORY TO SHARE?

We would love to hear about your personal breakthroughs while reading this book. Your stories inspire others and help us develop new workshops and support materials. Please share your experience by emailing **breakthrough@blindblaming.com**.

Include details about what changed for you, how specific processes in the book—like Revealing your personal Blame Loop story or applying the RCD Method™—supported your journey, and any unexpected insights you gained.

Your success stories move us forward in achieving our goal of helping 10,000,000 people discover their hidden truth. When you break free from blind blaming, we invite you to "Share your Breakthrough!" We look forward to hearing from you!

STAY CONNECTED WITH THE BLIND BLAMING NEWSLETTER

Want to deepen your journey past *Beyond Blind Blaming*? Sign up for our weekly newsletter to receive exclusive content, including downloadable versions of all the exercises and graphs from the book. Each week, you will receive an inspiring story featuring someone who has successfully moved past blind-blaming patterns to create more meaningful relation-

186 | BEYOND BLIND BLAMING

ships and authentic connections. These real-life examples show how these principles can transform lives and relationships.

Sign up today at **www.BlindBlaming.com/resources**.

LISTEN TO THE BEYOND BLIND BLAMING PODCAST

Join us each week on the Beyond Blind Blaming Podcast, one of the top-ranked personal development shows in the country. Every episode features intimate conversations with guests who share their transformative journeys from Blind Blaming to conscious living. From relationship experts to everyday people who have changed their lives, each story offers practical insights and inspiration for your growth. Search for "Beyond Blind Blaming" wherever you get your podcasts, and join our growing community of listeners committed to breaking free from blame patterns and building healthier relationships.

Check it out at **www.BlindBlaming.com/podcast**.

Or search for Beyond Blind Blaming in your favorite podcast app.

TAKING THE NEXT STEP

If you are ready to break through your current ceiling, your next move is crucial. Finding the right coach and mastermind group isn't only about making an investment; it's about making the right investment with the right people at the right time.

At **www.BlindBlaming.com/connect**, I have developed a systematic approach to matching you with the exact support you need. Let's break through, together.

About the Author

———

KEVIN **D.** ST.CLERGY IS A TRANSFORMATIONAL BUSINESS LEADER, mentor, podcast host, and author of the groundbreaking book *Beyond Blind Blaming*. After building and successfully exiting his own company, he now helps entrepreneurs, leaders, and individuals across diverse industries achieve breakthrough results by identifying and eliminating their hidden barriers to success.

In his book and through his podcast of the same name, *Beyond Blind Blaming*, Kevin introduces his revolutionary concept of "blind blaming"—the unconscious pattern of attributing problems to the wrong causes due to missing crucial information or insights. This pattern is "blind" because the real issue remains hidden from view, and manifests as "blaming" because humans instinctively seek to assign fault, even if it is to themselves. Through his work, Kevin helps people recognize and break free from these limiting patterns, unleashing their true potential for success.

As a strategic advisor and breakthrough specialist, Kevin's approach transcends conventional coaching. He focuses on uncovering root causes that hold people back, believing that true success requires alignment across all life dimensions—business, relationships, health, and wealth. His unique methodology helps clients see past surface-level challenges to discover solutions hiding in plain sight.

Drawing from his entrepreneurial experience and deep understanding of human behavior, Kevin leads high-impact mastermind groups and provides one-on-one guidance to those seeking transformative growth.

His philosophy is grounded in the belief that both success and struggles leave valuable clues—insights that, when properly understood, can illuminate the path forward.

Kevin's mission centers on empowering individuals to move beyond blind blaming and gain the clarity needed to achieve lasting results. He has demonstrated that when people finally see what's been holding them back, remarkable transformation becomes possible.

For speaking engagements, business consulting, breakthrough coaching, or to learn more about *Beyond Blind Blaming*, visit

www.BlindBlaming.com

or contact Kevin St.Clergy personally at

kevin@blindblaming.com

to explore how his expertise can help you achieve the success you deserve.